RESISTANCE
AND
RECOVERY

Also by Paul J. Curtin

Tumbleweeds: A Therapist's Guide to Treatment of ACOAs
Hidden Riches: Stories of ACOAs on the Journey of Recovery

RESISTANCE

and

RECOVERY

for

ADULT CHILDREN

of

ALCOHOLICS

Paul J. Curtin

Continuum • New York

1991

The Continuum Publishing Company
370 Lexington Avenue, New York, NY 10017

Printed in the United States of America

Library of Congress Cataloging-in-Publication Data

Curtin, Paul J.
 Resistance and recovery for adult children of alcoholics / by Paul
J. Curtin.
 p. cm.
 Reprint. Originally published: Delaware Water Gap, Pa. :
Quotidian, 1987.
 Includes bibliographical references.
 ISBN 0-8264-0539-8 (pbk.)
 1. Adult children of alcoholics—Psychology. 2. Adult children of
alcoholics—Rehabilitation—United States. 3. Resistance
(Psychoanalysis) I. Title.
HV5132.C87 1991
362.29'23—dc20   91–15597
                                                                          CIP

FOREWORD

This book reflects my own growth during the course of a year. A journey from knowledge and frustration to small increases in awareness and acceptance. I made a deliberate choice not to smooth over the rough spots. Acknowledging anger and sometimes unrealistic expectations is just as valuable as providing a theoretical framework for your consideration.

The week this book went to the publisher my mother was successfully operated on for cancer and we found out my wife was pregnant with our second child. Life created and life renewed. As usual, life's awesome richness exposes the poverty of my grand designs. It allows me partially to accept God's invitation to resign as Chairman of the Universe.

Wendy Ramsay typed this book and deserves a medal. Karen Curtin and Cordis Burns lived through the writing of each chapter and deserve a vacation. They, and all the people who so graciously read and commented on each draft, have my deepest thanks.

Paul Curtin
Syracuse, N.Y.
June, 1987

CONTENTS

I. INTRODUCTION

Recovery is not easy for adult children of alcoholics (ACOAs). The purpose of this book is to explore obstacles and opportunities ACOAs face on their journey to recovery. We will discover that this journey is very difficult and enormously threatening. As a result, resistance is both natural and inevitable. We will also discover that if resistance is addressed in an open and honest manner, this apparent obstacle will provide an opportunity to enrich and enhance an ACOA's recovery. A book on resistance may be contrary to the "feel good" atmosphere which often permeates the ACOA movement. This topic, however, must be addressed if we wish to legitimize the syndrome ACOAs develop and provide appropriate treatment. The ACOA movement has reached a state of maturity where we are now able to move forward and examine treatment and recovery. The admission of serious problems and concerns regarding the treatment and recovery of ACOAs need not be viewed as a threat to the work of those advocating for children and adult children of alcoholics. Rather it is a sign that the basic message, **children of alcoholics need and deserve help,** has been accepted and we can now move to the more advanced stage of what actually constitutes help and recovery.

A number of beliefs form the foundation of this book. The cornerstone is that ACOAs develop a unique, identifiable syndrome which requires specific treatment. This book will not attempt to justify this premise because a number of excellent books and articles have already covered that ground. Instead, it will focus on issues which arise in attempting to treat this illness.

The second level of belief deals with what is to be done about this illness. This book is based upon the premise that group therapy is the treatment of choice for ACOAs. (Exceptions being ACOAs who are active alcoholics, alcoholics with less than one year of solid recovery, those who have psychological or neurological disorders which prevent them from benefiting from group involvement, and those whose ego strengths are so low that they need supportive individual therapy.) This group therapy must also coincide with serious and in-depth participation in appropriate self-help groups (i.e, Al-Anon, ACOA support groups). Recovery requires a major commitment which cannot be achieved by simply attending therapy or a self-help group one night a week.

For our purpose, **resistance is defined as an attitude or behavior that opposes acceptance of reality, and awareness of self.** Often it is not a conscious opposition; it may be a lack of awareness of the unhealthy behaviors, unrealistic expectations, and incorrect perceptions developed by ACOAs as a result of parental alcoholism. Resistance causes problems and makes recovery a difficult, long-term process.

The chapters Hitting Bottom, Marriage, Family of Origin and Other Disorders describe areas which must be addressed, yet cause enormous fear and produce intense resistance on the part of ACOAs. The chapters Spontaneity, Intellectualizing, Lack of Interaction and Restricted Zones deal with the fear ACOAs have of developing healthy, intimate relationships based on openness, honesty and expressing emotions, while at the same time yearning to leave their loneliness and "connect" with others. This fear produces a resistance which creates a life based on attempting to prevent people from leaving instead of attempting to draw closer to them.

The final chapters, Relapse, Awareness and Recovery, show how resistance can actually be advantageous for ACOAs. They take the position that these obstacles are actually opportunities that can lead to acceptance and recovery. Resistance is viewed as a necessary part of recovery.

The ACOA therapy group provides the context for most of this book. In that environment ACOAs are called upon to create a community based on vulnerability, self-revelation and interaction with others. It provides an atmosphere where ACOAs cannot hide; they are forced to react to themselves and to each other. It is in group that ACOAs are generally most real. They can actually **experience** the journey towards intimacy as opposed to **chasing** intimacy in unhealthy ways. Though many of the examples used are from group therapy sessions, they also apply outside of group as well.

WARNING: THE SURGEON GENERAL HAS DETERMINED THAT THIS BOOK CONTAINS STRONG OPINIONS AND BIASES THAT MAY BE HAZARDOUS TO THE CONVENTIONAL WISDOM. It is my intention to provoke discussion. It seems as if a cottage industry has been developed that dispenses sugar and spice and everything nice about ACOAs. There is a tendency to be swept along by great numbers of people (ACOAs) who have just discovered a common bond and identity as well as the "answer" to their problems. As a result, enthusiasm replaces serious inquiry while clichés are substituted for thoughtful exploration. The euphoria of identification has its place, but the time has come to discuss the problems generated when the honeymoon of discovery turns into the resistance of day to day recovery. In my previous book, **Tumbleweeds: A Therapist's Guide To Treatment of ACOAs,** I said that the time had come to move from a description of the illness developed by ACOAs to a discussion of treatment needs. This book will continue from that point, discussing both recovery and resistance to recovery.

You are requested not to take this book too seriously. Taking a literal approach will only limit insight. During the period of time it has taken to write this book, many of my thoughts have changed. I can state with absolute certainty that 80% of what I say in this book is true. The problem is that I don't know which specific parts fall into the 80% category! Anyone can benefit from reading this book by turning it into a springboard to develop your own opinions. It is more important to develop your own well thought out opinions and positions, than to consider mine superior because they appear in print. The ACOA movement is in need of some healthy questioning and critical thinking. I invite you to leave all preconceptions at the door and have fun exploring.

II. MYTHS

Before we can talk about resistance in ACOAs, we must talk about resistance shown by the ACOA movement in general. This resistance takes the form of myths that develop from ACOA folklore. These myths result from the movement being stuck in the identification or honeymoon stage. The assumption is, "Once we have identified ourselves as ACOAs, everything will be fine". As a result of these myths, ACOAs have been misled regarding the depth of their illness, the difficulty of their recovery, the length of time that it takes, and their chances of success.

Myth #1 ACOAs are easy to treat.
This myth is based on the fact that it is relatively easy to get an ACOA to enter treatment. Once a person identifies himself as coming from an alcoholic family, an almost magical crystallization puts his life in a different perspective. It creates an initial enthusiasm for further exploration. Quite often ACOAs seek help soon after this initial realization.

While it is easy to get ACOAs into treatment, providing therapy and keeping them in treatment are very difficult tasks. Therapy involves challenging defenses and pathologies developed and perfected over 20, 30, 40 or 50 years. This process is enormously threatening because it attacks the very behaviors and defenses ACOAs have come to rely on.

It is safe to say that ACOAs enter treatment wanting to feel

4

better. Surrendering and undergoing a radical transformation are usually the last things they expect. They enter with an external focus. They are looking for something or someone to fix them. "Fix them" should not be interpreted to mean a fundamental change. Instead it should be viewed as wishing to rid themselves of the most pain and discomfort with the least amount of surrender. There is tremendous resistance to the idea that they are responsible for their own recovery and that their recovery will involve hard work, surrender, and transformation.

ACOAs are very difficult to treat. The depth of their illness is minimized by their denial of the reality of the need for change and by their belief that they have only a slight problem which requires a minor adjustment. **Treatment is often viewed as a luxury rather than a necessity.** As treatment progresses there will be battles in the areas of commitment to and responsibility for the discarding of well nurtured defenses. It is one thing to claim willingness to recover and quite another to be willing to do the work, feel the feelings and take the risks recovery entails.

Myth #2 **Coming from an alcoholic family is an asset**.

This line is generally given by speakers and authors who attempt to produce a catharsis in their audience under the guise of professional training and public information. Their spiel goes like this: *"Isn't it great we are all survivors! We have taken our parents' alcoholism and from that crucible, forged gifts which never would have been possible in a normal family. Our ability to work hard, our sense of the needs of others and our self-reliance have made us the chosen ones."* GIVE ME A BREAK! People who say this, especially those in positions of responsibility, should be invited to go back into the insanity of living with active alcoholics and see if they can develop even more gifts and assets!

Being raised by active alcoholics sucks! There is no other way to say it. This fact must be stated clearly and unequivocally. Without help there is no way for a child to avoid being damaged. Stephanie Brown's landmark work (See page 88) shows how parental alcoholism hinders a child's development from infancy. The implications of her work are so enormous and threatening that they are likely to be ignored. Being raised by active alcoholic parents creates a series of developmental disorders which produce chronic problems throughout a lifetime. This reality devastates the claim that ACOAs are fundamentally sound and merely need a few minor adjustments. Perhaps this myth has its foundation in

5

the resistance of the alcoholism field to viewing untreated ACOAs as impaired professionals?

There is, however, one class of ACOA that can truthfully claim to view their past with gratitude. This class is composed of those who have undergone a radical transformation based on a spiritual conversion. This makes talk of the past as either an asset or liability meaningless. It means acceptance and awareness, not justification and explanation. **Gratitude for the past is not the result of reasoning or the development of a new intellectual framework. It is a gift.** People who have been blessed with this acceptance have difficulty expressing it. It does not lend itself to words. Dag Hammarskjold came close when he said "For everything that has happened, thank you. For everything that is to come, yes."

Myth #3 **Mere knowledge is the foundation of recovery**.

ACOAs have an amazing thirst for knowledge about their illness. Obtaining theoretical knowledge is often more appealing than the process of recovery. Reading a book is not sufficient for recovery. Attending a conference does not replace participating in therapy. This book will not make you better. In fact, if you aren't careful, reading this book may hinder your recovery. (This doesn't mean I don't want you and your friends to buy a lot of copies. I'm not that much of a purist. Just take it with a grain of salt.)

It is dangerous to rely on the thoughts of others. In therapy ACOAs often become lazy and use the clichés of the movement. (i.e. "I'm not in touch with the child in me.") Instead of exploring who they are, they rely on the phrases and descriptions of others. They also use ACOA jargon in an attempt to identify with a peer group, when in reality it simply makes them more superficial. ACOAs live in the land of intellect. Thoughts are used to avoid feelings. **Information is valuable only if it brings them closer to other people and more aware of themselves.** Knowledge can also serve as an excuse to perpetuate unhealthy behavior. When an ACOA is confronted he says, "Well, we don't know what normal is." The phrase "I have to care for me" is used to justify irresponsibility. "Don't we all do that?" is used to avoid feeling. The list is long. Perhaps there is something we can do about this. The next time somebody starts a sentence with "Typical ACOA that I am..." interrupt him and ask if that can be translated into English and if he could please talk like a normal person!

Myth #4 ACOA recovery is a short term, fairly easy process.
ACOAs have been misled regarding the difficulty of recovering. They have been given the impression that if they remember the past, learn some new skills and have a nice cry, everything will be fine. Even better, they have been led to believe that this can be accomplished with only 8 weeks of treatment. This is not true. Their recovery cannot be self-directed and self-controlled based on what they read in a book or hear in a lecture.

This belief results in self-centered disclosure and superficial relationships. ACOAs disclose the most intimate details of their lives to virtual strangers. Talking about incest, parental violence and heartbreaking neglect becomes a standardized performance that does not increase intimacy and is just as isolating as silence. However, it is more dangerous than silence because it gives the **illusion** of intimacy.

It is sad to see childhood traumas turn into superficiality. When ACOAs congregate it often turns into a "Can you top this?" affair. It's as if they take turns listening to each other's tragedy. The very things that have harmed them become transformed into a passport that allows them to join a new social club! This process denies the reality of the events they so casually discuss at the drop of a hat and hides the poverty of their present lives. It is important to realize that ACOAs are not responsible for this state of affairs. It is a natural result of the movement's failure to provide more than a description and definition of the problem. We have failed to confront not only specific treatment issues but the reality of the recovery process as well. As a result we have left an entire population to attempt to heal itself.

It is no wonder that sentiment is chosen over reality; ACOA therapy is not always reassuring and soothing. Recovery is very difficult and threatening. The excitement of resolving the past is often used to avoid the emptiness of the present. **Therapy exposes the impoverishment of most current relationships and challenges ACOAs to create new ones.** The long-term process of getting to know oneself and creating healthy, intimate relationships in the present is not glamorous. It involves fear, risk and very hard work. It is also alien to the experience of most ACOAs. They will not embark upon this journey unless there are guides and structures. We have an obligation to develop a body of knowledge and experience to ensure that guides are provided and structure is given. ACOAs deserve more than the glitz and glitter they have been receiving. **They deserve treatment.**

Myth #5 **Recovery is assured for ACOAs.**

It is quite normal to talk about relapse and failure rates for alcoholics. It is understood that some alcoholics, although exposed to treatment, do not recover. When it comes to ACOAs, there appears to be a conspiracy of silence in this area. The unspoken message is that everyone recovers. Relapse, regression and termination of treatment against advice are never talked about. It's as if we finally discovered a Nirvana where everyone who enters treatment is a delight to work with, tries real hard and always recovers. Unfortunately, this is not the case.

For our purposes, recovery is defined as self-awareness combined with the ability to develop and maintain healthy, intimate relationships that are characterized by honesty, openness, vulnerability, expressing emotions appropriately, setting limits and recognizing needs. This is combined with an acceptance of the past as shown by awareness, appropriate mourning and forgiveness. These are not easy tasks, nor can they be achieved overnight. Generally it takes 3 to 4 years of therapy and self-help group involvement for recovery to occur.

Many ACOAs who enter treatment do not recover. They are unable to make the sustained, deep commitment that the recovery process entails. They are unable to see past the perceived threat to the rewards of recovery. ACOAs are asked to surrender the very things they believe are essential to survival. They are then given vague promises of future health, intimacy and joy. In order to achieve these they must make a quantum leap of faith into the unknown. They are asked to give up the system that has produced a somewhat bearable method of operating and instead face deep pain, intense anger and real fear all in the name of recovery. It is completely understandable when an ACOA decides to "pass" on the overhaul and settle for minor adjustments!

III. HITTING BOTTOM

Many ACOAs enter treatment with excitement and enthusiasm. Having finally discovered what is wrong with them, they believe the rest will be easy. Compared to the despair an alcoholic feels upon entering treatment, an ACOA could be considered to be experiencing a moment of triumph. This triumph is short lived and it is soon replaced with fear, confusion and anger. An ACOA has no conception of what lies ahead. It's as if he enters treatment wearing rose colored glasses. Resistance is found as the therapeutic process begins to remove these glasses and let in reality.

An ACOA generally hits bottom **after** he is in treatment; the alcoholic generally hits bottom **before** entering treatment. Though external events may have battered ACOAs into developing poor self-concepts, they still want to maintain control and call the shots. They begin treatment looking for more information, a different approach or some new answers. **They are not looking for a fundamental change in how they operate**. They want to learn how to make what they are already doing work. As ACOAs look for external changes, they discover that the more things change the more they remain the same. ACOAs must come face to face with the need for internal transformation.

Treatment equals increased pain. Resistance is a natural reaction to this prospect. An ACOA comes into treatment with a proven method of operating that is fairly effective even if it is isolating, semi-painful and unsatisfying. It has produced an emotional numbness that has effectively blocked all but the most intense pain. (Granted it also blocks joy, but to him that's a small

9

price to be paid.) Now he comes into treatment and we cheerfully announce that we are going to encourage him to give up his defenses and fully experience his emotions, including his pain. Of course he is going to be resistant! If he isn't, I would be worried.

Hitting bottom is an assault on an ACOA's self-sufficiency. Self-sufficiency is the very thing that has allowed a person to survive living with alcoholic parents. When all else failed (which it usually did) self-sufficiency generally saw him through. When this is challenged, it produces a sense of desperation and panic born of an ACOA's inability to use the old tricks and defenses. What used to work isn't working anymore. Control is slipping and a frantic attempt is made to keep things together.

Resistance is born of desperation, yet **desperation is essential to an ACOA's recovery**. There must come a time in the recovery process of ACOAs when they believe they may not recover, when they want to run away and forget the whole thing. They have to experience **at depth** that this is too much for them and they may not be able to do it. The results of facing this desperation are not assured. Many leave therapy before they face it. Others leave rather than surrender to it. Once self-sufficiency has been assaulted, the resulting pain can either lead them closer to others in a healthy manner or to a period of regression and retreat.

Many ACOAs view treatment as a luxury rather than a necessity. They attend, but never make a true commitment to the process. They are present but do not join. Their resistance stifles openness and prevents them from having the opportunity to hit bottom. They comply with the letter of the law. They do enough to keep themselves in treatment, but not enough to become vulnerable or make progress. Hopefully an external crisis may occur that cracks their facade. Most often these ACOAs merely put in their time. They remain in a defensive posture, closed to others and to themselves. Little progress will occur because protection is valued more than recovery.

An ACOA must be desperate to recover. Only desperation will force him to consider letting go of control. Progress occurs when the pain of giving up the unhealthy defenses and control is outweighed by the pain of keeping them. Unless an ACOA is committed to his recovery and his recovery is the primary element of his life this "blessed desperation" will never be reached. **Since his defenses are designed to avoid desperation, they activate automatically to reinstate control unless the ACOA places himself in a total lifestyle of recovery.** If he is not taking risks in therapy, reaching out to others on a daily basis, attending a lot of self help group meetings, praying and meditating, he will be unable and unwilling to face the desperation. An ACOA cannot "make" himself surrender. He can, however, make a conscious decision to take those steps which lead to a loss of control.

It will be useful to look at the difference between an alcoholic's entry into treatment and that of an ACOA. (I am assuming that an alcoholic who is also an ACOA will have at least one year of solid quality sobriety before entering ACOA therapy). Alcoholics often enter into treatment kicking and screaming, outraged that they are forced to stop drinking, go to AA and enter treatment. After a short period of time, most alcoholics grasp onto recovery and the promises of relief it offers. Conversely, as was said before, an ACOA enters into treatment in a moment of triumph. "I have finally found what I have been looking for." After a short period of time, many ACOAs begin to resist what is offered. (i.e. a focus on self, recognition of a need for others, and asking for help.)

Perhaps the difference lies in what people can expect in recovery. An alcoholic expects positive things: no throwing up in the morning, fairly solid bowel movements, increased job performance, more money available, fewer arrests, black eyes, and broken noses. This does not even include the mental and spiritual rewards of sobriety. The things I have listed come simply from stopping drinking and minimal AA attendance. They are immediate benefits of early recovery from alcoholism.

What can ACOAs expect in early recovery?

1. MARRIAGE PROBLEMS: ACOA therapy threatens marriages because it alters the balance and creates conflict. If an ACOA enters treatment because she believes she is unable to have healthy, intimate relationships, what does that say about the person who chose her as a spouse? Often the maintenance of a marriage depends upon an ACOA's continued sickness.

2. JOB DIFFICULTIES: Many ACOAs are over-achievers. They are unable to set limits, and employers often take advantage of them. Their attempts to cut back, work reasonable hours and have realistic goals create problems because people have come to depend on their exaggerated sense of responsibility.

3. THREATENED FANTASY REGARDING FAMILY OF ORIGIN: Often ACOAs view their families with a sense of

fantasy. They have restructured an unpleasant reality into a more acceptable one. Therapy invites them to see things as they are instead of how they wish they would be.

4. OUTBURSTS OF EMOTIONS: ACOAs repress and think away their emotions. Emotions are replaced by knowledge and understanding. The dam which harnessed emotion begins to crack once treatment is entered. It is not unusual for ACOAs to experience episodes of crying or rage which "sneak up" on them. Participation in therapy causes an internal commotion over which there is little control. They have sudden strong emotions which are both shocking and disconcerting, as well as disconnected from the present situation.

The recovery process requires a lot of courage on the part of the ACOA. This courage is often accompanied by resistance. This is only natural. After one year in therapy an ACOA is often in more pain than when he came in! He is fearful and doubts that the journey is worth it. It is normal to want to avoid this pain and anyone who doesn't display some resistance should be viewed cautiously. We are asking ACOAs to face what they have run from for so long. The key is to realize that the journey to surrender is a crooked one. To have begun the journey at all is a miracle!

IV. MARRIAGE

Though marriage was mentioned briefly in the last chapter, it deserves to be discussed in depth. Some of the most deep seated resistance in ACOAs is found in the area of marriage, or romantic involvement. ACOA therapy threatens marriages and romantic involvements on a number of different levels ranging from the relationship itself to the motivations for entering the relationship. Resistance will cover the spectrum from passive silence to active hostility. It would be quite easy to design an ACOA "pseudo-therapy" program which would avoid this topic or deal with it in vague generalities. However, **if ACOAs are to attain solid recovery, their marriages and romantic relationships must be explored**.

Another premise of this book is that **untreated ACOAs are incapable of having healthy, intimate relationships**. This is one of the main manifestations of their illness. It does not take an ace logician to take this premise a step further and state: *If ACOAs are incapable of having healthy, intimate relationships, they are also incapable of having healthy, intimate, romantic relationships*. ACOAs are often quick to embrace the theory that they have "trouble" with relationships. They readily admit the problems they have had in the past. They can provide a detailed list of past hurts, slights and mistakes. The common theme is that even though mistakes were made in the past, **this** relationship is different. The risk involved in examining past marriages and relationships is nothing when compared to the risk in examining current marriages and relationships!

Many ACOAs seem to have a compulsion to be romantically involved. (Another percentage is obsessed with having **no** involvement). There is a real fear of being "alone". It is interesting to note that this concept of "alone" ignores all other types of relationships and shows a lack of self-awareness. It is common for a member of an ACOA therapy group to justify entering another unhealthy romance with the excuse "I was just so tired of being alone". The person is then surprised when his fellow group members angrily retort, "What about us? What about your friends in Al-Anon? Just because you're not having sex doesn't mean you're alone!" This concept of "aloneness" devalues all other relationships. It is an insult to the other members of the group who are attempting to have a relationship with that person. The value of non-romantic relationships is ignored in the quest for the perfect mate.

A person must be free to leave a marriage before that person can stay in the marriage with freedom. This is one of the foundations of a healthy marriage. **It is acknowledgment that marriage involves a gift of self rather than an attempt to create a self.** ACOAs tend to define themselves through externals. Often a marriage or romantic involvement becomes a way of obtaining self-worth or self-identity. "If I have a partner I am not a failure or undesirable." "If I have a partner I will have someone who will appreciate me." "If I have a partner I won't have to work so hard." The true statement is "If I have a partner I won't have to look at myself." **The lack of a spouse or partner means that ACOAs must come face to face with themselves.**

Usually marriages and romantic involvements are not seriously addressed by the ACOA in therapy until after an extended period of time. In fact, early in the course of treatment marriages are viewed somewhat idealistically. The person believes entering therapy will most definitely improve the marriage. (It's interesting to note that the word "improve" is used most of the time, even when the word "save" would be more appropriate.) After all, now that he is getting help, things will have to get better. As the other group members begin to examine their marriages, a pinpoint of panic begins to develop. The process of evaluating a romantic relationship realistically, making informed decisions and acting on those decisions is alien to most ACOAs. Remember that we are talking about a population that has little or no experience with healthy marriages, and few healthy role models to imitate. They believe that they are lucky to have anyone! They have been taught to accept what has been given to them, be grateful for what they have and to hold on for dear life because they probably won't have another chance to be with somebody. Even listening to others discuss marriage in an open and honest manner creates discomfort. It's as if ACOAs are being forced to encounter the very thing they wish to avoid.

Along with the panic, there is an intuitive sense that the member is in the same boat as his peers. At this point resistance rears its head with more intensity. He fights making the jump from marriage in general to his own marriage in particular. Instead he develops a sense of uniqueness. He believes his marriage is different or that there is no pressing need for him to talk about his romantic involvement. This happens automatically with little, if any, awareness on his part. It is a normal reaction to a threatening process which requires vulnerability and risk. When a marriage is examined with the help of peers in a group setting, the system of assumptions, unspoken rules, unexpressed desires and ignored needs must be challenged. This process seeks to replace the old system, where the person often settles for whatever is given, with a system in which the person makes deliberate choices. **The ACOA is called to take responsibility for the state of his marriage**. This is not responsibility in the realm of blame, but responsibility that requires a decision to remain or leave. It means developing a manner of operating based on action rather than reaction.

Our organization is often referred to as The Divorce Factory. There is a rumor that we get a commission for each divorce or breakup that happens in our practice. It is easy to see how this misconception occurs: people enter treatment hoping to improve a marriage and after two years may realize that it has to end. They find that they can't stay passively in one place. If they look at their marriages critically it will cause problems at home, but if they don't take a hard look, their fellow group members will nail them for not being open. They are literally caught between a rock and a hard place! They are being forced to make a decision. They are being deprived of the opportunity to operate by default, merely drifting as events unfold. They must take a stand.

Resistance is a rational response to these unattractive alternatives of painful awareness and angry confrontation. It is an attempt to forestall the inevitable. Resistance should be viewed as natural and in some sense beneficial since it allows an ACOA to remain in treatment while he gains the resources and necessary foundation to look at this area. (This is another reason why short term therapy is not the best choice for ACOAs. The dynamics of relationships take a good deal of time to get to and are easily avoided. Awareness and action cannot occur in a 12 week program.) In one sense, the therapist can be grateful if resistance takes the form of honest anger and open hostility, since it provides something to work with. Unfortunately, one of the most common expressions of resistance is silence followed by departure. Patients frequently leave therapy rather than face their marriages openly and honestly.

Resistance and commitment are not mutually exclusive. An ACOA's honesty about his anger or resistance is an outward manifestation of his commitment to the therapeutic process and his recovery. By inviting ACOAs to examine their marriages or romantic involvements critically we are precipitating major traumas and must be aware of the responsibility that this entails. We should never underestimate how difficult this is for the ACOA. Though these issues must be addressed, the approach should be one of invitation rather than bludgeoning.

Some specific forms of resistance in the area of marriage and romantic involvement deserve to be listed separately. This list is by no means all-inclusive. It merely represents some frequently used gambits in ACOA group therapy:

1. "WE'RE JUST GOOD FRIENDS". This allows an ACOA to be obsessed with a member of the opposite sex and still claim in group that he isn't romantically involved. He can spend most of his free time phoning, spending time with and planning to spend time with his target. However, since there has been no sexual intercourse (yet), it need not be discussed in group. He can then blithely say "I have every intention of bringing this up in group if we decide to start a relationship." (In what category does he place this endeavor that consumes ninety-nine and forty-four one hundreths percent of his free time?)

   In another version, two group members become sexually attracted to each other. Since ACOA groups have (or should have) a requirement that members not date each other, one can see how it could tax the imagination to get around it. The method most commonly used is for the members to form a "special friendship". The couple meets to rehash last night's group; they meet weekends for bike rides and long walks; they become confidants and turn to each other for help.

16

While all this is going on there is a corresponding decrease in their interaction during group sessions. There is also no mention of their "special friendship" in group. Anger and vigorous denial categorize their responses upon confrontation. Group members are accused of having dirty minds and not being understanding.

The reason for the vehemence of the response is that the couple has been "caught", their secret exposed. What they have been hiding is no big deal. It is simply more familiar for them to operate from a sexual framework because in reality they often don't know how to have relationships with people outside of that realm. Hopefully they will come to see that theirs is a universal ACOA condition. If they had been open from the beginning about what was happening, they would have become closer to their peers rather than more isolated.

Both of these examples require an active effort on the part of the ACOA to keep his activities secret. He has a sense of guilt about his behavior, that may be disguised by blaming his secretiveness on the perceived hostility or jealousness of the group. His use of these relationships can be viewed as external self-medication, because, in reality, it is one more attempt to run from himself by using a sexual relationship to give him a sense of self. This is the real secret he is trying to protect.

2. SILENCE. The ACOAs who use this can sit in group a long time and never mention their spouses or partners. Everyone knows they have one, yet that person never becomes a topic of discussion. They give the impression that even though they are married, they are on their own. The spouse has become a part of the landscape. "I have a house, a nice lawn, a new car and George." When attempts are made to get the ACOA to be specific regarding wants, desires and wishes for a marriage, the response is a blank stare followed by a list of chores the member would like to see the spouse do. The ACOA will have difficulty even being aware of personal needs such as caring, attention, and support. The ACOA has given up on (or never expected from the beginning) marriage as a mutually enriching relationship. There is no sense of shared vulnerability and openness leading to mutual growth. Instead the marriage becomes more constricting and the expectations more external as the ACOA becomes more

numb.

One should be aware of how this member reacts when someone else's marriage is the topic. Usually there is silence coupled with a physical rigidity. The silence may be broken by a one liner that chides the group for "picking" on the other person. A sense of impending doom is the motivation behind this reaction. "Are they going to pick on me next?" The member tries to become invisible while hoping for the discussion to switch to another topic. It is also not unusual to find the member absent the week after marriage (his or others) was addressed. This is a more obvious and extreme attempt to distance himself from a painful topic.

This area is very threatening because it involves more than mental and emotional aspects; it also involves societal and financial issues. Are there some ACOAs who should not enter the recovery process? It's dangerous to call into question the fundamental elements of a person's life if he does not have the internal or external resources, to change. Some ACOAs have adjusted to their syndrome. Their lives are familiar and semi-comfortable. Though they are emotionally isolated and lack true intimacy, they are stable and function in a variety of roles. What happens when a 60 year old female ACOA with no job skills or financial security becomes aware of the poverty of her marriage? Sometimes I wonder if what is required to attain awareness, transformation and self-actualization is worth the disruption it causes in people who are too firmly entrenched in the ACOA syndrome. These questions do not lend themselves to easy answers, but they must be asked.

3. NO WAY! This method is quite refreshing. The ACOA simply says "No, I'm not going to talk about my marriage. There is nothing wrong." The manner in which it is said can be sickenly sweet. "I really would like to discuss it if there was a problem, but we've worked on all of our issues and our marriage is super." It can also be a little bit abrasive. "If you think I'm going to let you tear apart my marriage, you're crazy." Either way the message comes through loud and clear.

As treatment progresses the member may become more open. He may learn that "No Trespassing" signs are usually erected to keep people out and protect a problem. A relationship that can't be talked about is not worth having. If he is lucky, his fellow group members will risk his wrath and continue to press him. If he isn't, his peers will buy his routine and he will drift away from them. He will eventually find himself in a situation where he doesn't fit in, both at home and in group.

4. THE PROGRESS REPORT. This is used by people who announce major events in their marriage or romantic involvement weeks after they occur. This technique is also good at raising the collective blood pressure of the ACOA therapy group. Here are two good examples:

I. Q. "Is that an engagement ring?"
A. "Yes".
Q. "Does that mean you're engaged?"
A. "Yes".
(At this time various sighs and mutterings are heard in the room.)
Q. "Why didn't you tell us about it?"
A. "Well we only decided to get married two months ago and I wanted to wait until I got the ring before I announced it."

II. (This takes place five minutes before the end of group.)
"I know we're supposed to share things so I want you to know I let my wife move back in with me and I'm very excited."
Q. "Isn't she an active alcoholic?"
A. "Yes".
Q. "Didn't you say she was hitting the kids and making life miserable for you?"
A. "Yes, but she hasn't had a drink in three weeks and we're seeing a marriage counselor."
(At this time various explosions are happening throughout the room.)
Q. "Why didn't you tell us you were seeing a marriage counselor and were even thinking about letting her move back in?"
A. "I thought you would be upset and anyhow I knew what you would say. See, you're acting just the way I knew you would."

The best that can be done is try to show the member the

19

distinction between informing members about his life and letting them into it. The key word is **process**.

5. IT'S YOUR FAULT. This ACOA wants the group or the therapist to take responsibility for his action in a marriage. He begins a fight with his spouse by saying "Paul said we should look at this." He explains a decision to separate with "The group said it might be a good idea." When things get tough or painful, he always finds a way to bail out. He never has to take a stand. He is just following the advice of people who should know what they are doing.

This is particularly tough to deal with because the action he is taking appears to be healthy. It is important to remember the difference between compliance and acceptance. Major changes, such as separation that results from ACOA therapy, are usually hard fought actions following hard work and risk. Glib agreement should be a warning sign that the full impact of a decision has not been realized. The above examples show a person complying externally to recommendations while showing no inner transformation or progress.

Marriage and romantic involvement are difficult areas. They can also be very fruitful. A decision to be open and honest allows the ACOA to address some of the fundamental issues of his recovery. Each ACOA must face these issues if recovery is to progress. Resistance comes with the territory. It is important for the therapist and group members not to become discouraged. Persistent, firm invitations to examine this area will develop a momentum that will not be denied. Will the patient remain and accept the invitation or will he leave rather than face reality? That is the key question.

V. FAMILY OF ORIGIN

We need not discuss the journey an ACOA takes when he leaves the world of fantasy and sees the reality of his childhood and family. This area has been well documented throughout the ACOA movement. It is a moving and beautiful process. It unleashes powerful emotions and can provide a sense of freedom. It is filled with excitement and is one of the major factors in the astonishing growth of this movement.

Problems arise when ACOAs attempt to divorce the reality of this awareness of their past from their present, day to day living. One way to put it is, "Now that you've seen the truth, what are you going to do?" Early on in group, the ACOA is quite willing to talk about his family. It is usually in terms of the past, however. His present relationship with them is seldom addressed. This eagerness to discuss past family experiences fades quite rapidly as therapy progresses. He realizes he is faced with a challenge. He must make decisions and take action. When action is expected resistance will be found! When the topic of action comes up the newly aware ACOA generally fears the worst. "Do you mean that I have to fly 2000 miles back to my home town and find my father? The last time I saw him he was in a drunken rage and threatened to kill me if he ever saw me again. Now you want me to tell him how enraged I was at him, but as a result of therapy I've been able to let it go and replace it with forgiveness?" Of course it would be foolish to propose such a thing here. Instead, let's look at some smaller and more manageable actions. These will not be things to do as much as things not to do.

1. PHONE CALLS. One ACOA was so excited about her new discovery. At age 30, she had become disenchanted with her twice a week phone calls to her active alcoholic parents. She would call after supper and be mad at her parents' negativism, slurred voices and continual repeating of the same questions every three minutes. She always hung up feeling empty and angry. She was very excited about her new solution. **Instead of calling her parents at 8 PM when they had been drinking, she would call them at 8 AM before they started!!**

    She was a bit surprised when her group didn't share her excitement. "Why call at all?", they asked her. It had never occurred to her simply not to call! This twice a week exercise in misery had never been questioned. Now she discovered she had an opportunity to act her way toward recovery. She could set limits and act on her own behalf. (This is easier said than done; generally there is a gradual weaning process before this false obligation is stopped all together.)

2. VISITS. The bi-weekly dinner with active alcoholic parents is not fun. Approached with a sense of dread, it generally causes a lot of conflict between the ACOA and his spouse. Neither wants to go, but duty calls. When asked to list the enjoyment he gets from this, he doesn't know where to begin because there usually is none. His reasons take the form of negatives. "I don't want to hurt them." "I'm all they have." "It's not that bad." "They would be destroyed."

    The challenge for the ACOA is to have dinner with his parents when **he** wants to. The goal is to teach him how to set up a decision-making process which does not rely solely on his own misperceptions. If he has decided to go, he can then be helped to see that he has the power to structure the visit by changing time of arrival, length of stay and developing other options. He now realizes that he has power over all these things. He no longer has to be a prisoner of ritual.

3. HOLIDAYS. "We have it all figured out, Christmas Eve we spend at my husband's parents' house because they don't drink before midnight mass. We then go to my parents' for

Christmas morning because they are too hung over to start drinking while we're there." Sounds logical to me. The concept of holidays being restful and refreshing is a foreign one to most ACOAs. Generally they are times of frantic motion, depression and anger. Not only does their childhood come back to haunt them, but in one sense they realize that they have never emotionally left their childhood.

ACOAs often resist starting their own holiday rituals, but this activity is vital if they wish to be free. Making the decision to celebrate a holiday in a healthy way is a sign of growth. It is a recognition that their "actual" family is one that they are creating with their recovering friends or with their spouse and children. There is more for them in this new community than in their family of origin.

4. PROBLEM SOLVING. This ACOA's job is to keep his family of origin going. He is a cross between a banker, Dear Abby and an employment counselor. He always has an answer and usually doesn't hesitate to give it. He is filled with anger because his advice is not only ignored, but is also unwelcome. In fact, it gets so bad that his family "detaches with love" and puts limits on their interaction with him! (They probably learned how to do this from the hundreds of alcoholism books and pamphlets he had strategically planted around their house in the hope of enticing them into treatment.)

This type of behavior denies the reality of the disease of alcoholism. Its premise is that if the externals are taken care of, the alcoholism will go away. ACOAs resist the idea of letting their families hit bottom. It is remarkable how ACOAs switch roles from rescuer to victim and back to rescuer. The irony is that by attempting to avert the various crises that alcoholism causes his family of origin, the ACOA helps perpetuate the very illness he is trying to save them from!

Money is an important issue for ACOAs to examine in therapy. ACOAs frequently claim poverty at the same time they are making regular contributions to their families. We have had people ask for reduced fees so they can continue to support active alcoholics. This "support" is not readily talked about. Mentioning the subject in group is generally met with anger. The reason is that **stopping enabling is not easy**. These ACOAs have become irresponsible. In attempting to rescue their families of origin, they have ignored their own obligations. They become angry when they are confronted and held financially accountable for themselves.

5. TRIPS AND VACATIONS. If an ACOA works 50 weeks a year and only has a 2 week vacation, why would he spend it staying at his alcoholic parents' house? In case you haven't guessed, the answer is "Because we always do!" In our ACOA groups, people have gone to Florida, driven cross country and gone camping with their active alcoholic parents. Upon their return, they talk about the great time they had. Five minutes later it changes to a good time. A bit later it wasn't all that good. Finally, they are really angry and start ranting about how they knew it would be terrible but they went anyway.

The key question is, "How much is your sanity worth?" The money spent on staying in a motel instead of your parents' house will be less than the amount spent on Maalox if you don't! Opting for a week at the lake with your new friends will be more relaxing than a week at the ocean staying with your family. **Vacations need not be more stressful than work!**

These may be simple problems, but they are not easy. The keys are honesty, planning and the willingness to be an adult. For these issues to be resolved ACOAs must take a stand. They must be responsible for their own happiness and actions. They must learn that their parents do not entrap them; they entrap themselves.

The first step is for an ACOA to say to himself, "I do not want to do ...". This is the first step toward freedom. The second is to say, "I don't have to do ...". These steps involve nothing more than self-honesty. However, once they are taken, **action must follow**. If the ACOA fails to take action and change his behavior, he will regress. He will be living a lie. He will be consciously acting in a way contrary to his own recovery.

The second step involves planning. The principle is that **the ACOA does have power**. He can decide what he wants to do based on his own needs and desires. His main activity need not be a quest to make people happy who are incapable of being happy. Activities can be accepted or rejected based on their benefit to his recovery. It is important to remember that this is not a solitary process.

24

Planning and identifying needs should involve the ACOA's fellow group members. He has had little experience or practice with these activities. **The process used is usually more important than the decision made.** Through his acknowledging how distant he is from his alcoholic family, he will be brought closer to others and be allowed to create a new family based in recovery.

VI. SPONTANEITY

It is somewhat surprising that a chapter on spontaneity has been included in this book. Spontaneity is seen so infrequently in ACOA therapy groups that it is easy to forget! This is not a case of ACOAs' resistance being expressed by action. It is an example of resistance characterized by inaction. This lack of spontaneity is not just a result of educational deficits. While a small part may be attributed to a lack of knowledge ("I didn't know I could say that." "It never occurred to me to speak.") much more is the result of fear and anger.

Lack of spontaneity is primarily a method of control. For our purposes control is defined as the attempt of ACOAs to structure themselves, their relationships and their environment in such a manner as to reduce the necessity for healthy dependence and vulnerability. It is easy to see why lack of spontaneity is such a vital component of this defense system. By giving only measured, considered responses, ACOAs can limit their vulnerability. Instead of **having** relationships they become actors in a play. Each response and interaction is part of a carefully choreographed script, designed to give the **appearance** of intimacy. The relationship is created by blue smoke and mirrors. The play is merely a play; it has nothing to do with reality. The actors dance around the real issues and their true selves with little understanding of who they truly are or where they are going.

ACOAs have tremendous insight. They often get a sense of what is happening with a person before the person is aware himself. They are usually great sources of insight regarding other people and external situations. This intuitive "radar" was developed by necessity in childhood. It allowed them to "read" a situation almost instantaneously and produce one of a variety of predetermined responses. This tool was developed, not to bring them closer to people, but to protect them by giving a response either to end a conversation, defuse an explosive situation, or get something they may have needed. While this tool was beneficial because it allowed the child to survive a hostile environment, it also had a great cost. The cost is the loss of spontaneity, openness and vulnerability. As adults, they still operate based on what they perceive the situation calls for rather than their own needs. It provides for little meaningful interaction or sharing.

In ACOA therapy groups this lack of spontaneity is reflected in two main areas:

1. RELATING TO OTHERS

Often ACOAs sit in groups simply "turned off". They know that the person who has been talking for 10 minutes is full of hot air, yet they remain silent. It's as if they say to themselves, "Charlie is talking, so I can zombie out for a while." Other times they are suddenly furious at another member. Instead of saying something, they wait for the anger to pass and then silently attempt to analyze what happened.

The ACOA's refusal to interact shows a lack of commitment, not only to the other person, but to his own recovery as well. He is choosing to remain in his own world. This aloofness can be sugar coated: "I didn't know how to say it." "I didn't want to hurt her feelings." "I didn't know we were allowed to say whatever came to mind." However, this does not give the full story. To a large extent these rationalizations are just a smoke screen. **The real issue is that the ACOA is not willing to take the risk of engaging the other person.**

It is not a question of simply not knowing how. Often ACOAs have a burst of spontaneity when they first enter group. This is because they don't really know the other members and are eager to do things right. This spontaneity disappears once they become invested in the other members and realize how their recoveries are intertwined. The closer they get to people the fewer risks they are willing to take. They stop taking risks and being spontaneous in order to protect themselves. It can be viewed as one hand washing the other. "I won't give you a hard time, so you won't give me one." This aloofness can also be viewed as arrogance. "I can see you acting like an idiot, but I'll just sit back and watch you flounder." (I know too well that arrogance is often a mask for fear. It still does not change the fact that this behavior is very unattractive.)

It's as if a tacit agreement has been reached where no one wants to rock the boat. Each member moves cautiously. It reminds me of soldiers working their way through a minefield, each one watching where he steps while keeping the others in sight, but not too close. The ACOAs remain in their own world avoiding interactions because they are either afraid of conflict or don't want to expend the energy that reaching out would require. Often it is difficult to get a reaction from ACOAs; in group the most outrageous announcements are often met with silence. Granted there might be a few heads shaken, eyes rolled and sighs uttered, but it's rare to hear a member exclaim "I'm sick of your whining. Stop it!"

Here's an interesting experiment. Next time an ACOA wastes a half hour of group time giving yet another variation of the same boring theme that has become his trademark, give the group a quiz composed of a few simple questions. (This can be done outside a group as well.) a. Was anyone bored? b. What were you doing when he was talking? c. Why did you ask him those questions? (Often when a member goes round and round chasing after his tail, other members feel an obligation to play 20 questions instead of saying "Let's move on.") d. Why didn't you say anything? You will find out that almost everyone in the room was fed up after the first 2 minutes. During that time, other members were composing shopping lists, having mental fights with their bosses, counting the flowers on the rug and a variety of other things. No one was being honest.

This repression of spontaneity regarding insight into others has an amusing side effect. It creates a room full of ACOAs who look like a modern dance company. They appear to be following a choreography of John Cage music. During a member's 15 minute soliloquy of the "poor me's" they shift and they twitch. Their legs flail away, first crossing and then uncrossing. They slump down in their chairs then shoot straight up. Heads are scratched and hands are rung. Their faces go through a variety of contortions from pout to grimace and then to blandness. All of this is a physical manifestation of their internal struggle. This struggle is based on the knowledge that they are aware of something not being right and the fear they have of actually saying so.

The resistance to spontaneity is a struggle for control. A battle is going on inside ACOAs. One part of them is fearful and wants to keep things safe and superficial. Another part truly wants to have meaningful relationships and be open to others. The outcome of this battle will be significant. It will determine whether ACOAs' gift of insight into others will continue to be used as a barrier to keep people away or whether it will be used to draw them closer to others.

II. RELATING TO SELF

Lack of spontaneity also causes problems in the area of self-awareness. In their efforts to give guarded, correct responses and do relationships "the right way", ACOAs become isolated from the very thing they are trying to protect: their true selves. They lose sight of who they truly are. It can be said that they become their defenses. They begin to operate based on what they believe the situation calls for, instead of what they truly feel. This emphasis on reaction allows them to shift the focus onto others while they remain blind to themselves.

Each time an ACOA gives the answer he believes someone else wants, he denies his own identity. He becomes a chameleon, changing identities with each shift in the environment. He surrenders his own identity in exchange for surface calm. Taking a stand in a relationship is frightening. It means creating the potential for conflict. Addressing and resolving conflict is a fundamental aspect of healthy relationships. ACOAs come from an environment where conflict is never addressed in a healthy manner. They view it as something to be avoided.

"I don't like this." "I don't like to do that." "That makes me mad." "I'm really happy." These sentences seem so simple. In reality, they are major leaps in the recovery process of ACOAs. Each time they are uttered they become affirmations of an ACOA's worth, signifying that the ACOA is a person with needs, preferences and limits. These are the essential foundations of healthy relationships.

As the ACOA recovers, he becomes free to make mistakes. Statements and activities need not be repressed until they are figured out. The ACOA allows other people into the **process** of his life. He learns that mistakes are essential to his recovery. The more out loud his mistakes are, the more worth they will have. Mistakes are no longer viewed as a devaluation of self. The ACOA need not fear being the only one in group to have a particular emotion. He need not worry about being mistaken when he confronts someone, because he has been given the gift to see that his value as a person is not dependent upon his performance.

29

Self-acceptance leads to spontaneity. The ACOA need not deny what he is thinking and feeling. This results in self-awareness instead of self-censorship. When he is not afraid of his thoughts and feelings, he is then free to know them. Hiding from others results in self-delusion; being spontaneous results in self-awareness. The ACOA gives others the gift of his unprocessed thoughts and reactions. This is done in a spirit of acceptance and with the realization that they collectively may know him better than he knows himself. In turn they give him the gift of enlightenment through their care and insight. The whole process starts with the ACOA taking the risk of being spontaneous. This is the essence of recovery.

It is now time to look at instances of lack of spontaneity. (These examples have been chosen with slow deliberation, careful planning, deep thought and a particular emphasis on what you would find useful.) While they will be used in the context of ACOA group therapy, they are not limited to that arena.

1. WONDERING. This is used when the ACOA silently wonders about what is happening. He sits in group and has a mental conversation with himself: "What is he saying? Am I the only one who feels this way? What will happen if I say something? I wish she would shut up. I wonder if I should talk about something when she is done. I see Charlie looking at me. I wonder if he is mad about something." If one looks at this person, there is often a blank look on his face while all this is going on inside. By not letting others know what he is thinking, he is actually withdrawing from them.

   Asking a direct question such as "Are you mad at me?" is quite threatening. Silent wondering is perceived as safer because the ACOA does not have to become vulnerable. He can stay inside of himself and be protected rather than initiate an interaction.

   Possible response:
   A. Ask the person what is going on when he remains silent.
   B. Ask why he didn't give other members the courtesy of telling them what was on his mind.

2. AND NOW I'D LIKE TO INTRODUCE. . . ACOAs tend to preface things they are afraid to say with qualifiers and

explanations. The process goes like this:

An ACOA is listening in group. She gets a flash of anger when she watches the person talking about doing something he had promised not to do. Wanting to be spontaneous, she starts. "Well, I have to interrupt, and I really don't like doing it, but I have to do it so I will. Now I don't want you to get mad at me when I tell you this because it's really hard for me to do. I may be wrong, but I will feel bad if I don't say . . ." The rest of the group gets so mad at her for beating around the bush that she doesn't even get a chance to say what she wanted to say in the beginning!

This technique of qualifying allows ACOAs to lessen their commitment to their statements and insights. It enables them to present strongly felt emotions and firm beliefs as mere asides. They can gloss over any potential conflict before it actually occurs. It allows them to have some sense of interaction with a minimal amount of vulnerability.

Possible Solutions:

    A. Interrupt as soon as qualifying starts.

    B. Ask what emotion the person is feeling. (Generally fear)

    C. Tell the person to start over and be direct.

3.   DO UNTO OTHERS. This ACOA is very spontaneous regarding his reactions to others. The problem is that all of his participation is other-centered. He can be counted on to exclaim "I'm glad you said that." "That makes me mad." "I feel closer to you." He is usually the first one to give a reaction. **All that is shared in his reaction to the recovery process of others.** The missing ingredient is self-revelation. The ACOA does not have to focus on himself if his main activity is to focus on others. It is easy to say "I'm real mad that happened to you," when another member shares an incident of neglect in his childhood. It is more difficult to allow that sharing to trigger memories and emotions regarding neglect in the ACOA's own childhood and for him to say "That happened to me too.". Members will soon discover what the ACOA likes and dislikes about them, how he will react in a given situation and what he looks for in others. However, they will know very little of who he is and what is happening in his life.

Possible Solutions:
  A. State that the person has done well responding to other people and invite him to share about himself.
  B. Ask the person to initiate something in group rather than provide a reaction. (This will usually provoke anger.)

4. I'LL HIDE AND YOU SEEK. "I don't know." is followed by a deep sigh and helpless shrug. This signals the game is afoot. The other ACOAs react to their cue. "Maybe it's this. Maybe it's that. Did you ever consider. . ." They automatically jump in to get the person off the hook. It becomes **their** responsibility to do **his** work. While this is going on the member can sit back and calmly ponder, then reject, each theory offered. "No, I don't think so. That may be what I'm feeling but I'm not sure. No, it definitely isn't that, but thanks for trying." It becomes a ritualized game, which degenerates into theory and intellect without meaningful sharing.

In another version, the ACOA talks in two sentences or less: "My wife spent one thousand dollars without telling me. She said she wouldn't do that." This is followed by silence. Group has a vague idea of what's happening, but 95% of what the ACOA is really thinking and feeling has been repressed. A deliberate, pasteurized condensation is given instead of a spontaneous expression of emotion. Once again the group jumps in and tries to pry details and emotions from him.

This kind of resistance is one of the biggest time wasters in ACOA groups since many ACOAs love to "help", and are more than willing to spend 20 minutes of group time trying to get the member to be more open and revealing. Of course, while this is going on the other members don't have to look at themselves. The member doesn't have to take responsibility for his own lack of sharing while the others can benefit from shifting the focus on him. Everyone can say he participated and yet no one has truly said anything. Everybody wins!

Possible Solutions:
  A. Group members can formally announce they will stop playing the guessing game.
  B. When the person says "I don't know" one can say "OK, if that's all you are going to do, let's move on." (That's called

the "stew in your own juices" approach.)

5. LOOKING FOR MR. RULE BOOK. Spontaneity is often repressed under the guise of trying to do the right thing. Members repress intense emotion because it's not their turn to speak. They will claim they wanted to confront another member, but didn't think it was allowed. They will hide something they are involved in because they don't know if it is appropriate to bring it up in group. Of course if ACOAs take the risk and actually attempt to validate these misperceptions, they will find them to be inaccurate. **Claiming not to know the rules reinforces unhealthy behavior.** Initiating efforts to find out and follow the rules leads to recovery. Often deliberately ignoring rules is even better!

Another version of this is Mr. Therapy. He puts on his therapy face as he enters the room. His talk is full of ACOA theory and jargon. He really tries to **do** group. He scrunches up his face to be intense. He sits on the edge of his seat, stares the speaker in the eyes and nods his head approvingly. His responses come straight from the latest book he has read. There is very little spontaneity in him. A classic scene was the time a member said to Mr. Rule Book "I'm sick of you acting like a pompous know-it-all." His response was, "I can see why you are saying that since we ACOAs sometimes hide behind our intellect. Thank you for pointing that out to me." The member's immediate response, which will live forever in our Spontaneity Hall of Fame was "Up yours!"

Possible Solutions:
   A. Remind them that it's not a question of correct or incorrect, it's a matter of real or phony.
   B. Ask if they talk and act differently at dinner than at group. (Usually they are more real at dinner than when they are trying to "do" group).
   C. Instruct them to talk like "normal" people and not use clichés and jargon.

Spontaneity is essential. It reveals to others what is actually happening internally instead of what the ACOA thinks should be happening. As ACOAs recover, they discover that they don't have to pretend anymore. It is no longer necessary to pretend they are not mad, to pretend they are happy or pretend they understand. They do not have to "do group" perfectly and manufacture intensity. **Spontaneity means freedom**. ACOAs become free to make mistakes and be real. Relationships with their peers do not depend on **correct** responses; they depend on ACOAs becoming aware of their true selves and sharing who they are.

VII. INTELLECTUALIZING

Contrary to outward appearances, there is more to ACOAs than their thoughts, theories and intellectual insights. The problem is that this world of intellect is a prison from which few ACOAs escape. A landscape of ideas, beliefs, understandings and rationalizations prevents them from reaching their emotions and thus becoming aware of their true selves. This fortress of the mind has been erected as a natural response to the trauma of being raised by active alcoholics.

It is not difficult to see why ACOAs have come to rely on thoughts and ideas instead of accepting feelings and emotions. Growing up in an alcoholic family places a child in an on-going atmosphere of tension, unpredictability, broken promises and unmet needs. It is an environment where anger, fear, hurt and confusion are constant companions. The child is left to fend for himself emotionally in a situation where there is little emotional honesty or stability.

The child begins to build a barricade of denial and understanding to protect himself from the effects of alcoholism. "I really didn't want it" protects him from his mother's failure to give him a promised gift. "Dad must be real sleepy" explains his father's passing out. "They had a lot to do at work" covers up the hurt of his parents missing the awards ceremony. As this distortion of reality continues, a distortion of self also takes place. The child begins to deny the anger and hurt. He views himself as either not having needs or as having needs that are unimportant compared to those of his parents. In an effort to decrease the pain and cope with his aloneness, the child "shuts off" or numbs more and more of himself.

When he reaches adulthood, this retreat into intellect is almost complete. The ACOA has successfully constructed a life which has very little disappointment or acute pain. In doing so he has also created a life of fundamental loneliness. Often he is unaware of the price he is paying, because years of reaction and compensation to alcoholism have blinded him to his true self. Emotionally he is aware of less and less as the numbness takes more and more of him.

One of the main tasks of ACOA group therapy is to develop the ability to identify and express emotions honestly and appropriately. It is easy to see why there is great resistance to this process. ACOAs have learned early that acknowledging and feeling emotions involve too much pain, while sharing emotions with others involves too much disappointment. To avoid these problems, ACOAs have developed an intellectual screening system. The system serves a dual purpose. It protects them from the internal pain of their emotions by creating a framework of denial, rationalization and suppression of needs that blinds them to their true selves. It also protects them from external disappointment by limiting interaction to "safe areas" while never making their true selves vulnerable.

There is a tendency to create ACOA therapy groups which have teaching and understanding as their primary goals. Such an intellectual approach is playing into the hands of the illness. It gives the surface appearance of recovery, while continuing the ACOA's fundamental isolation. ACOAs are great understanders. They are more than willing to "learn" about their illness. There is a remarkable willingness to "share their knowledge" at a moment's notice. This pursuit of knowledge is yet another attempt at self-adjustment based on intellectual knowledge. It implies that ACOAs are fundamentally sound and only need more information in order to fix themselves.

Education and theory are useful in the early stages of recovery. They provide an incentive to get help and are valuable in establishing a commonality of background and feéling of belonging. However, once an ACOA therapy group is underway, information and theory become weapons the ACOA uses in his struggle to avoid intimacy and vulnerability. **It is easier to discuss the reasons for unhealthy behavior than to experience the consequences of that behavior**. It is more pleasant to discuss the phenomenon of ACOAs having trouble with marriages than to face the pain of having to leave your own. It is preferable to discuss your difficulty with emotions than to tell a fellow group member you are mad at him.

It is important to keep in mind our definition of recovery. Recovery is "Self-awareness combined with the ability to develop and maintain healthy, intimate relationships that are characterized by honesty, openness, vulnerability, expressing emotions appropriately, setting limits and recognizing needs." It does not call for theorizing. **ACOA group members are called to develop relationships; they are not asked to develop a theory of relationships**. They are called to develop an awareness of self that is richer than merely defining themselves by means of a theoretical framework.

If one were to draw a map of an ACOA's recovery, it would show a journey out of the land of intellect and into the world of emotions. The goal is to share what is being felt; not what is being thought. An ACOA's retreat into intellect is the result of chronic hurt and disappointment. Asking him to leave his fortress is threatening on two levels. In the first level we are asking him to experience the pain and anger of the past which he has fought to suppress, ignore and deny for so long. On the second level we are asking him to be vulnerable to people in the present, thus exposing himself to new opportunities to be hurt. We are asking him to discard a life-long method of protection from both himself and others

It is important to remember that ACOAs do not live in their heads because they want to. They did not sit around at age 9 and say "I'm tired of being hurt; I think I'll intellectualize in order to numb the pain". This defense developed in conjunction with their own development and is very deep seated. Intellectualizing will be a constant problem in ACOA therapy groups. In one sense it is the gateway to almost every issue an ACOA will have to address. It is often very frustrating to deal with because it is so difficult to penetrate. The key is to realize that fear is the foundation of this defense. It is the care group members develop for each other that allows them to see-that this defense is no longer necessary.

The following are some methods of intellectualizing found in ACOA therapy groups.

1. WHAT GOOD DOES IT DO? The premise is that if an emotion is valid, it must have a desired affect on another person or situation. "Why should I get mad? It won't make

any difference." Understanding of the situation replaces emotion, "I won't get too happy because I know it won't last." **Knowledge of a situation, or of another person, blinds them to the reality of their own emotions.** This form of intellectualizing is also used to hide the fact that their own needs are often unmet. "How can I be mad at someone who has a disease?" "I knew he wouldn't follow through." "I really didn't expect anything." These are attempts to restructure an unpleasant reality rather than become aware of that reality. This approach diminishes an ACOA's sense of self. He becomes an adapter rather than an actor. The price of thinking away his pain is that he loses his personal foundation. He then lives in a world of rationalization which bars him from self-awareness and self-acceptance.

2. WHY DO WE DO THAT? This is a common method of diffusing tension and escaping meaningful interaction. It turns a moving encounter with another person (or with one's self) into a safe, theoretical discussion. The following is a good example because it involves trying to get the therapist to bail out the ACOA and protect his emotions. *I feel horrible, my life is a mess. (At this point tears are starting.) There isn't enough time in the day. I'm always frantic. I can't ask for help, yet I can't stop trying to do everything and be perfect. (Sobs come now.) Oh, I don't know. (Short silence while he regains composure.) Tell me, Paul, am I like this because I had to work hard and overachieve in order to get my parents' approval? (Happy now.) You know, I just realized that I'm so overresponsible because I had to take care of my brothers and sisters while my parents were drinking. You know, I really do wonder whether or not my brothers and sisters were affected in the same way as me. (Looks pensive and stares into space.)*

Focusing on the reality of his life has given way to a theoretical understanding of it. Legitimate pain resulting from unhealthy behavior has been turned into a game of Trivial Pursuit. When the emotions got too vivid a circuit breaker was thrown which automatically turned on the intellect. It is interesting to note that when this is reviewed with the ACOA, he often has no awareness of having switched off his emotions. (This is an example for the need for active group members and an active therapist. **Immediate confrontation** allows the ACOA to begin to develop an awareness of this behavior.)

3. LET'S FIGURE OUT WHAT'S WRONG WITH YOU. This occurs when ACOA group members provide a resisting member with their theories of his problem. It is a well practiced ritual. The group member looks intense, gives one sentence statements, has lapses of silence followed by "I don't know". The other group members say things like "Maybe it's ...", "I think it could be ...", Did you ever consider ...", "You had better look at ...". Members are usually very persistent. The game can last upwards of 30 minutes!

The main problem with this game is that no one really wants to play. Like bloodhounds on a scent, they are propelled by their own programming. It is a sign of health when one can say, "I don't want to do this". It is important to ask group members when they are trying so hard to help. They need to look at what they are feeling when they are being helpful. It is not unusual to find that their "help" disguised anger at, or boredom with, the resistant member. There is also a sense of relief because while they are composing their theories about the other member they don't have to look at themselves. They are able to **appear** to be participating, while in reality they are offering decoys. At that level of interaction they only offer their theories and explanations, not themselves. There is little vulnerability or openness.

4. I KNOW IT'S NOT GOOD FOR ME. This is one of my all time favorites. If an ACOA admits that what he is doing is wrong he can then continue to do it! Here's an example: A group member says: "I know I shouldn't be sleeping with my friend's wife and I need to stop." The response is "That's a real good insight, I'm glad you shared that." By admitting that what he is doing is not good for him, he has successfully blunted the group's response. Unfortunately, this intellectual admission still leaves him blind to 95% of the reality of his actions.

The member can then explain why he needs to stop and how bad he feels about the whole incident. The other members congratulate him for this self-confrontation and everyone is happy. The member can now continue his affair, knowing that he has discussed it in group, and that people will support him while he gets ready to end it. In reality, the ACOA is incapable of truly seeing not only what he needs to do, but why he is even in the situation to begin with. His activity is based on instinct and reaction. His lip service to "wanting to do the right thing" covers the fact that he has no idea who he is or why he is involved in the affair. It is easier to admit unhealthy behavior than to be aware of the reality of that behavior. Discussing a problem does not always lead to change.

The other group members are also experiencing difficulties. ACOAs have been raised on hints and innuendos. Instead of pressing someone to be specific regarding his intentions, they attempt to "read between the lines" and draw their own conclusions as to the person's intentions. They make numerous unspoken assumptions and many unsupported guesses. They assume that since this particular behavior has been discussed, the member will change it. They don't usually ask "Are you going to stop?" and "When are you going to stop?". In this case, mere discussion about generalities may actually prolong the unhealthy behavior.

Such questions are asked as ACOAs get healthy. "Have you stopped?" is a sign of further health. It means they actually have the courage to return to a difficult subject. They are beginning to expect action rather than discussion. They want to see the member change, or at least develop awareness, rather than hear him talk. They are moving from the realm of intellect into the world of action.

5. LET ME ASK YOU THIS. Though some legitimate questions are asked by ACOA therapy group members, most questions are methods of hiding. There is more to them than a simple request for information. They generally fall into these three categories:

    a. **Hostility and anger**. These questions resemble those of a prosecuting attorney. They are filled with righteous indignation and cannot be answered without a sense of shame. "I just want to know when you will do more than just sit there and look like a cadaver." It seems to me that there is more than a little hostility in that statement! It's designed to attack rather than interact. It puts the other person on the spot while the questioner can hide and share little of himself.

    b. **Other focused**. These questions are designed to help others. It is safer to help others than it is to ask for or accept help. It allows a semblance of interaction without the vulnerability. On a more subtle level, a member will ask questions of others in order to learn about himself. Instead of admitting that he is in trouble with his marriage, he'll ask questions of others in an attempt to figure his marriage out in secret.

c. **Irresponsibility**. The ACOA believes the therapist and group will give him answers. These answers will give him a plan to follow. Since the plan is actually someone elses, if it fails, he has someone to blame. Always be cautious of questions such as "What should I do?", "What do you want me to feel?", "Why am I doing this?". It is very easy to take the responsibility for someone else's recovery. Very often ACOAs will be glad to give it to you.

One of the main factors in successfully dealing with intellectualizing is the health of the therapist. If the therapist is uncomfortable with emotions, the group will not be led into that area. Instead they will remain in the area of safe discussion. Emotions will be discussed, not expressed. If the therapist is unsure of himself, he will often break silence and begin to teach rather than wait for the discomfort of silence to produce action. He will be eager to answer questions and discuss theories; often providing the group with answers rather than allowing the members to find their own.

The key is to use knowledge as a tool rather than a weapon. Knowledge can be used to put the interaction of ACOAs into perspective. It should not be used to replace that interaction. An ACOA's capacity for insight and understanding is a gift. In therapy he will learn to use that gift in a self-enhancing rather than a self-defeating manner.

VIII. OTHER DISORDERS

Many ACOAs enter group with other disorders in the areas of eating, gambling, work, sex, depression or neurological problems. There is a tendency to focus on "ACOA issues" and not address these other areas. I believe this is a mistake because it is almost impossible to make the distinction between ACOA and non-ACOA issues in a person. It is my belief that a combination of genetics and environmental stressors play a large part in the development of "other" problems. It is impossible to treat one and not the other. The ACOA movement has rightly criticized the mental health field for treating the symptoms instead of the core issues of ACOAs. It is just as important that we not ignore these other problems when we address the ACOA syndrome. **The claim that the ACOA syndrome is a primary illness should not be used to perpetuate other pathologies.**

ACOAs' recovery entails their developing healthy, intimate relationships with each other. This is not possible if the other disorders of group members are not addressed. It would mean ACOA group members are attempting to develop openness and honesty while ignoring obvious problems. It becomes a living example of the Emperor With No Clothes fairy tale. In reality, members have to work very hard to appear oblivious to these outstanding problems.

In group it is not unusual for ACOAs to have tacit agreements with each other. There is an unspoken pact that each member will be allowed one "ace in the hole". That ace will be one disorder, problem or issue that no one will ever address! This brings to mind the mutually assured destruction (MAD) approach taken by the United States and the Soviet Union. Group members co-exist, realizing that if they go after someone else's untouchable disorder then theirs will be fair game. As a result, they are reluctant to address the protected problems of others.

A lot of non-verbal DO NOT DISTURB signs are posted in ACOA groups. Members seem to know instinctively what topics to avoid, and the thought of violating these rules creates terror. ACOAs were raised in families where the main task was to ignore the obvious and deny reality. Alcoholism was the center of family life, yet it was rarely acknowledged as such. As children they learned to keep their perceptions to themselves. When they attempted to acknowledge reality, they were often told they were mistaken or they were simply punished. They developed an instinct to identify the areas where a person is really vulnerable. This instinct is then used to guide them away from areas of conflict. (It also can be used as a brutal weapon in an ACOA's bi-annual explosion which results in a savage "fight to the death" with a loved one.)

Addressing the disorders of others is seen as a hostile act. It is seen as something that an ACOA would never do if he were attempting to build a relationship with someone. He believes it would cause too much pain and drive the other person away. For him, relationships depend upon not making waves or causing trouble. It wouldn't be worth the problems that he believes would occur if he addressed these issues. This spotlights the fear that ACOAs bring into relationships. They constantly struggle not to say the wrong thing. They act in a manner which is designed **not** to draw them closer to others, but to **prevent** others from leaving them.

The following disorders and issues are frequently encountered in ACOA therapy groups.

1. EATING DISORDERS. There are 2 levels of denial in regard to eating disorders. The first is an initial reluctance to confront the issue. A 300 pound ACOA asks members how they see him. They in turn talk about his personality, his emotions, his interactions with them, and how they really care for him. No one says that they see him as fat, but this is their primary conception of him! His obesity permeates their perceptions, yet it is never addressed. Their relationship is based on a fundamental lack of honesty.

43

The same holds true for anorexic weight loss. The members are alarmed at the thinness yet no one says anything. Instead, they often offer compliments regarding the member's choice of clothes or ability to stay away from desserts, or treat the member as a fragile child who may break if confronted. It is likely that many members may be revolted by that emaciated appearance. They then berate themselves for being so judgmental and try even harder to ignore it.

Therapists are often unwitting accomplices in this denial. Many are reluctant to confront the issue and make appropriate referrals. Eating disorders have only recently been viewed as requiring specific treatment, so treatment centers are scarce. Even when adequate treatment is available, many ACOA therapists are still reluctant to make the referrals. The tendency is to exclude eating disorders from an ACOA's treatment plan. This is due not only to ignorance of available resources, but also because the therapist is uncomfortable with the issue. **Therapists must be willing to address eating disorders instead of waiting for the ACOA to give permission.**

The second level of denial is follow-through. A member may attend Overeaters Anonymous or Weight Watchers for 6 months with no weight change. This fact will usually not be mentioned. Members will rarely ask if the ACOA has been following his food plan (Or if he even still has one). It is taboo to ask the member to talk about his eating, or to actually say that he doesn't look any different. Even though these may or not be "proper" or informed questions and statements, the point is that they are on everyone's mind! To think them and not ask is to be dishonest with the person.

2. GAMBLING. Characterized by loss of control, it is both rarely addressed and is also looked upon with some amusement in ACOA therapy groups. This is a particular problem because there appears to be a correlation between alcoholism and compulsive gambling. It is important not only to focus on the gambling of ACOAs, but on the possible compulsive gambling of their parents as well.

Gambling brings us to an area of money. Money is not a neutral topic for ACOAs. It is filled with emotion and unspoken significance. Viewed as more than mere currency, it generates issues of control, security, obligation and self-

44

worth. There can be many opportunities to discuss money during the course of a group. It is usually the job of the therapist to "give permission" and encourage this discussion. The issue of money calls for ACOAs to break their established patterns of secrecy and self-sufficiency. They must examine their attitudes towards money. Do they cling to it while worrying about losing it or throw it away without any concern at all? A lot will be learned by looking at how they budget and manage their money especially in terms of flexibility, awareness of options and developing alternatives. They will have the opportunity to discover how much money they actually need, or desire, and make appropriate plans. They can explore whether they use money as a means to define themselves, or simply as a tool.

Some ACOAs are very responsible about paying for their treatment. Others resent having to pay. They procrastinate, and are indignant when limits are set. It is a major event when an ACOA has to ask for financial help through a reduced fee or admits financial problems in general. His financial situation must be explored. Often this is very frightening because it may be considered a forbidden subject which touches upon painful areas. However, addressing it brings the ACOA to look at areas such as self-definition, security, failure, success, emptiness, and self-sufficiency.

3. WORK. From an employer's point of view, ACOAs are ideal employees. They work long hours with incredible determination. They work harder than most and set very high standards, but are silently resentful about a perceived lack of recognition. Eventually the resentment turns into anger at themselves **which leads them to work even harder**.

The employer's job is to tell ACOAs how valuable they are to the company. He should tell them that he cares for them and that he considers them an important part of the corporate family. (If he does this he will get solid performances and never have to worry about giving raises. In fact, the ACOAs will probably tithe 10% of their salaries back to him in appreciation! The only problem is that he will have to let them go after 3 years of employment, just before their rage explodes!)

Compulsive working, definition of self through employment, unrealistic expectations, under-employment and absence of satisfaction are among the problems ACOAs face. Often these areas are protected by a variety of excuses and situations which make change difficult. ACOAs often view themselves as victims. Their work is not appreciated and the fact that they are working harder than others is also not recognized. A resentful pride in their performance substitutes for a sense of satisfaction. The reason for this is that the external framework of a job cannot substitute for the internal development of a sense of self.

4. SEX. When sex is discussed in ACOA therapy groups, it is more on a general than on a personal level (I must confess that I'm not sure if it's due to the nature of ACOAs or the nature of myself as a recovering Irish-Catholic therapist). There is usually an absence of real vulnerability when sex in the present is discussed. There may have been a great deal of success addressing past sexual traumas on a feeling level, but current sexual activity is more closely guarded.

The concept of sexual addiction is beginning to receive more attention from therapists. It is an area that must be raised in ACOA therapy groups. When a member brings up a sexual obsession, compulsion or dysfunction, the initial outward reaction of group members is one of support. They congratulate him for talking about it and say that they feel closer to him. The topic is usually not brought up again. This process allows the ACOA to disclose something about himself, the group to be nurturing and the issue to go unresolved.

A general rule of thumb is that when a sexual problem or compulsion is raised, the group's reaction is not totally honest. They act as if there is an imperative to be encouraging. Although they may be repulsed, disgusted, angered, or afraid, they will respond with "I'm so glad you shared that." They may be terrified because they do the same thing, but their response will be "It must be hard for you to open up like this." There is no spontaneous reaction. They seek to give the "correct" response. The belief is "Since the person struggled so hard to talk about this, who am I to be mad at him?"

It is interesting to note group member's responses to homosexuality. They tend to go to great lengths to avoid the topic. If they can't ignore it, they claim that a member's sexuality is not a problem for them, and in fact, it isn't even an issue. Of course this isn't true. It is an emotionally charged issue since ACOAs are ensnared in all or nothing, black or white approaches. They believe their only options are to be totally accepting or totally repulsed. It is difficult for ACOAs to believe that their reactions can cover a wide range of combinations. Even if they do believe that there can be variety in their attitudes and emotional responses, it is very rare for them to be honest about these responses. This denial applies not only to sexual orientation. The same process goes on regarding race, physical handicaps or any other major difference. In group, ACOAs get the opportunity to experience the fact that honest reactions are the prelude to openness which then leads to acceptance.

5. PSYCHOLOGICAL DISORDERS. Some people are constitutionally incapable of benefiting from ACOA group therapy. They may be suffering from major psycho-pathology disorders such as schizophrenia, temporal lobe epilepsy, low functioning, borderline personalities, or major depressive disorders. These problems may not be picked up during the intake and assessment period. As a result, these people may be placed in group by mistake.

    After a short while, it becomes apparent that something is wrong. They may talk incessantly with little relation to the topic. They may talk primarily in clichés, repeating and rewording what others have said. There may be a sense of thinly disguised rage, barely held inside, or outbursts or emotions that are out of proportion to the situation. It is not unusual to see extreme self-centeredness and inability to make contact with other group members.

    I am not referring to ACOAs who exhibit isolated instances of these behaviors. The key is a continual pattern which is sustained, unchanging and deep seated. It seems that everyone in the room is aware of such problems, but it is hard to address them directly. Sometimes both group members and therapist alike will ignore them.

    Group members simply write off the incessant rambler. They will wait patiently for him to stop his talking and then resume their therapy session as if he didn't exist. They will pity the person who emotes at the drop of a hat, or they will sit in terror of the human hand grenade and go out of their way to placate him. They know that these people are "different", but they assume that either their perceptions are incorrect, or there is nothing they can do about it. It is essential that the therapist take an active and aggressive role. In most cases he will not have the expertise to make a complete diagnosis. However, he is capable of recognizing that this member appears to have something more than the ACOA syndrome, and making a referral for a psychiatric evaluation.

It is vital that the organizations providing ACOA therapy have a working relationship with a psychiatrist/psychologist who is familiar with alcoholism and alcoholic families. The therapist must use this resource as a valuable tool, since he will frequently encounter ACOAs who need more help than he has to offer. The therapist must be competent and healthy enough not to treat those he is incapable of treating and not to let inaction compound the problem of inappropriate placements.

The essence of this chapter is not so much the disorders themselves, but ACOAs' reluctance to confront them honestly. Their rule of thumb, that it is easier to ignore a problem than to address it, results from a lifelong habit of ignoring the obvious and not making waves. They "work around" someone rather than interacting with him. They believe it is more fruitful to give "the party line" instead of an honest response. While they are affirming someone on the surface ("Just because you take a bath only once a month doesn't mean I don't care for you as a friend."), they are pulling away physically and silently removing themselves. ("I have to breathe through my mouth whenever I'm near him.")

Recovery entails a building of relationships. These relationships involve honesty and interaction. ACOAs must become vulnerable and participate in each other's lives. The depth of their interaction is a mirror of the depth of their recovery. Not addressing these problems is a disservice, not only to the person with the disorder, but to the ACOA as well. By ignoring the obvious he increases his own isolation. He settles for relationships that are guarded and shallow. The risk taken by addressing a disorder is both an affirmation of self and the other person. It shows that there is no real reason for either secrecy or shame.

IX. LACK OF INTERACTION

Recovery is not a solitary process; it requires interaction and self-awareness. **The interaction required for recovery is the very same interaction that ACOAs' defenses are designed to avoid.** The barriers to interaction used by ACOAs are nothing more than a natural consequence of being raised by active alcoholics. This puts resistance in a different light, since it is generally not a conscious activity.

ACOAs generally have encounters rather than interactions. While interactions can be described as a joining of people in which each person is vulnerable and deeply touched, encounters can be considered as a series of surface maneuvers designed to obtain something while maintaining a safe distance. In general, ACOAs' lives can be described as a series of encounters designed to achieve a desired goal with a minimum amount of vulnerability. These encounters result in an isolation from others and being trapped inside a self of which they have little awareness.

Instinctive calculation characterizes the lives of most ACOAs. They seek either the path of least resistance or the route of decreased vulnerability. They base their calculations on their perception of their environment, their view of the people involved, what they want to attain and what they don't want to lose. The last factor is the critical one. Their encounters are based not so much on attaining something, as on protecting or trying to avoid something. This leads to a life which is both defensive and reactive. (Surface appearances to the contrary, this also applies to

49

ACOAs who act super-irresponsible, zany or spend-thrift. These behaviors are designed to avoid the depths of disappointments and fear of planning.) This life of reaction allows them to live in unawareness, blindly trudging forward. A life based on action requires awareness and willingness to accept and embrace who they really are.

Lack of awareness leads to lack of trust. The problem is not so much with trusting others as it is with self-trust. I am not talking about ACOAs not trusting their skills, competencies and performances. (Usually there is a combination of excessive pride and insecurity in these areas.) This lack of self-trust is most profound in the areas of emotions, instincts and perceptions. It is in the areas that relate to self-worth and self-acceptance that there is the least amount of self-trust. As a result ACOAs are "living on the edge". One mistake, an error in judgment or a simple misperception will have enormous consequences in their eyes. It would not simply be a mistake, **it would be a devaluation of self**. Instead of **doing** something wrong, they instead **become** wrong. Since they have no sense of self-awareness and did not receive adequate nurturing and affirmation during their childhood development, their self-concept is defined by their actions and the reaction of others. They act as if they are attempting to forestall being discovered as a fraud, both on the inside as well as on the outside.

It is no wonder that ACOAs have encounters rather than interactions. Those instinctive calculations that limit vulnerability also serve to defend the one secret that ACOAs protect with awesome tenacity and frequent unawareness. **That secret is the fundamental belief that they are essentially unlovable and not intrinsically valuable**. To open themselves to others and to interact with them constitute powerful threats to ACOAs. It means that the secret that they have been hiding for so long must be faced. This involves a leap of faith into what they perceive to be the darkness of pain and rejection. Yet it is usually pain that precipitates that leap! The pain of staying in the same place must become greater than the anticipated pain of vulnerability.

ACOAs yearn to make this leap of faith into self-awareness and interaction. They yearn to be deeply touched by other people and to touch them in return. This spark is well hidden and often denied, but it is there nevertheless. This speaks to the value of the ACOA therapy group. It is the awkward, fumbling, terrifying attempts at interaction with other group members, the very thing ACOAs have been trying to avoid, that will give them the best chance to have that spark ignite. The unity of the group gives an ACOA the opportunity to experience the acceptance of others, when self-acceptance is unavailable. The accomplishments and failures of his fellow ACOAs in group provide invitations to risk that yearning and allow it to grow.

The methods ACOAs use to resist meaningful interaction are varied and colorful. Watching month after month of such resistance often makes it easy to forget that **they do yearn to interact**. Here the therapist's knowledge of ACOA theory comes into play. ACOAs usually have to be taught the principle of interaction. The therapist cannot simply sit still and wait for them to interact, because ACOAs do not have the data base, or frame of reference, to develop interaction skills on their own. They must be guided and encouraged until open interactions become natural. Encounters must be reviewed and then replayed with hindsight as if they were interactions. ("Let's do that again, but this time try to be a bit more real.") The therapist must rely on the fact that he has more insight into ACOAs than they themselves have. ("I bet you really wanted to say 'You're full of shit', when instead you said 'I'm not sure I see the validity of what you're saying so I'd appreciate it if you would rephrase it'.") He must also ask questions designed to reveal to ACOAs what was truly happening with them. ("What was it like when he said that to you?", "Why did you respond that way?")

It's time to look at examples of ACOAs' lack of interaction in the group therapy setting. It is important to remember that they stem from a combination of fear and lack of knowledge. Both of these aspects must be taken into consideration. All the teaching about interaction will be superficial unless the fear and terror are addressed and resolved. Working on fear and the terror of other people will not be fruitful unless new ways of interaction are provided at the same time.

1. ...AND THAT'S IT. An ACOA wants to bring up a topic, but not really deal with it. He semi-fulfills the requirement of disclosure, but shuts the door on interaction. Other members will have to overcome his consciously stated desire to end the discussion. His statements often begin with the phrase "I just wanted to let you know ...". An example would be "I just wanted to let you know that I decided to get divorced. My spouse took the kids, packed the furniture and left me with an empty apartment when I came home from work. I'm

feeling hurt and mad, but I've taken steps to protect myself legally. I think I've covered just about everything, **so that's it."**

2. LET ME SEE. This is where ACOAs sit and try to figure out what they think and feel about what another member has said to them. A prerequisite to this is the stifling of any spontaneous reaction. It represents wariness; they doubt both their own perceptions and the motives of others. It is more important for them to give a correct response than a real one. The purpose is not to share themselves, but to achieve a desired result.

3. THE COP OUT. This is shown by a lack of aggressiveness regarding self-knowledge. The ACOA accepts his initial reaction of having no thoughts or feelings about another member or issue. He settles for "I don't know." Instead of working to find out what is happening inside of him by asking for help, he becomes lazy and silent. As an ACOA becomes healthy his "blankness" becomes unacceptable to him and he becomes committed to self-awareness.

4. THE WAIT. An ACOA has tons of things he needs to talk about but he sits silently and waits to talk about them. He often forfeits his group time, claiming "There wasn't an opportunity for me to bring it up." He has no conception of working on his own behalf or making his needs known. This allows him to blame the therapist or other group members for his work not getting done. As a group gets healthier such behavior decreases. It is exciting to see three or four members anxious to do work expressing their need to talk and then interacting and negotiating with each other to see that their needs are met.

5. IT WASN'T THAT IMPORTANT. ACOAs don't bring up in group major things that happen in their lives. They believe that these issues are unimportant; they should be able to handle them on their own. Discussing them is simply not an option. This is an example of the screening process used by

ACOAs. Instead of sharing the entire mosaic of their lives, they only present what they consider to be significant. The tendency is to be self-sufficient as much as possible. However, the key to interaction is allowing your life to be an open book to group members, not parcelling out information in bits and pieces! Too much of the color of life is lost if the members only share censored stories about problems already resolved.

6. I KNEW YOU WERE GOING TO SAY THAT. ACOAs won't raise an issue because they are afraid of the groups' response. It is preferable to keep secrets and avoid conflicts than to have honest interaction. A general rule is that hiding things from group members usually results in more anger than would result from sharing those secrets.

7. THE THIRD PERSON. In group ACOAs often talk **about** another member instead of **to** him. An example is "I wanted to let everyone know that I'm mad at Ron, and I think he hasn't been honest with the group." Instead of "Ron, I'm mad at you because I think you haven't been honest with me or the other members." It is much easier to make the announcement in the first example than to have the interaction the second example requires.

When a member says he is mad at the whole group, it usually isn't true. In reality, the anger may be directed at only 3 or 4 other members. When he states that he believes "people" aren't sharing in group he usually has specific people in mind. The therapist must help the ACOA be specific. This allows him to attempt to interact with the people who have made him angry.

8. THE SILENCE. This is very common in ACOA therapy groups. It results from a number of circumstances.

a. **Boredom** - Instead of saying that they are bored, often members will tune out and sit in silence until the member who is boring them is finished talking.
b. **Punishment** - A member has been confronted or had a fight with another member so he sits in silence and pouts.
c. **Twist in the wind** - After a member shares something

painful or takes a major risk, he is often greeted with silence. The other ACOAs have been touched so deeply by what has happened that their only reaction is to keep quiet. Instead of sharing what is happening inside of themselves, they are frantically working to regain composure and control. This self-absorption on the part of the other members leaves the ACOA who shared slowly twisting in the wind.

9. REFUSING TO FIGHT. There is no greater way to give ACOA group members the finger than by refusing to have a legitimate, fair fight. When members refuse to fight with each other, they are saying the relationship isn't worth the possible conflict. Anger is a component of any healthy, intimate relationship. When the member says "If you are going to act like that, I'll just not say anything," he is closing the door on interaction. It is a very smug and condescending method of operating.

10. THE FINISHED PRODUCT. An ACOA presents group members with a result rather than a process. He announces that he quit his job, gives the reasons for quitting and discusses what emotions he felt. This is all done after a decision has been made. The ACOA is generally surprised when he is confronted about this. The idea of sharing the **process** of his decision-making is alien to him. In all probability he has never had an experience of a calm, open, decision-making process which is shared with others. As he progresses in his recovery, he will discover that the decision is actually secondary to how it is made. If he approaches the process with an open mind, invites others to help, and has self-acceptance, a particular decision may be wrong but not harmful. The key is whether it is an opportunity to move closer to people or whether it is another attempt at adjustment based on self-sufficiency.

11. EMOTIONAL DISHONESTY. This is when members give what they believe is a "correct" response instead of an honest one. An ACOA who is particularly obnoxious

announces he is leaving group. Members respond by wishing him well and saying how sad they are to see him go. It would be a great day, both for themselves and the person leaving, if they were actually honest. "You were disruptive when you were here and I'm happy you won't be coming back."

12. FOLLOWING THE RULES. Many members attempt to do the minimal amount of work that is required. Their actions are designed to protect, rather than expose themselves; they give the appearance of participation while actually eliminating vulnerability. They will do their homework, give reports about their lives and respond cautiously to other members. They can then point out how they are trying to "do group" the right way, but in reality no one can point to anything real about them and they continue to hide behind their masks of performance.

13. I DON'T WANT TO INTERRUPT. Sometimes ACOAs act in group as if they are at a self-help group meeting. They sit silently while each member has an opportunity to share his experience, strength and hope. They stifle spontaneous interaction because it is not their turn to speak. They'll let a member ramble on because they wouldn't want to take the risk of interrupting. They devote their time to silently analyzing what the member is saying instead of interacting with that person.

True interaction requires vulnerability. It involves taking risks and making mistakes. **Mistakes are vital to healthy relationships**. They signify that the ACOAs have gained enough trust to believe that they won't be banished for saying the wrong thing. When ACOAs have gained self-worth, they realize that if a person leaves because he was mistakingly confronted, that is his problem, not theirs. Since recovery is not a solitary process, the community of an ACOA therapy group is designed to force interaction. ACOAs have a two-fold task: to resolve the fear, hurt and anger regarding past attempts at interactions and to develop the skills to interact in new, healthy ways.

X. RESTRICTED ZONES

Most ACOAs enter treatment with at least one major issue that is absolutely untouchable. They have amazingly well fortified defenses to protect these areas. "Thou shalt not invite me to look at this." is their motto. These "restricted zones" are not necessarily the result of conscious decisions on the part of ACOAs. It is not unusual to discover that they exist outside their consciousness. Whether conscious or instinctive, the restricted zones produce great problems for the ACOAs when they are broached.

These untouchable areas generally fall into two categories, those requiring change and those requiring painful awareness.

1. CHANGE - In this area the ACOA realizes that if a particular issue is addressed, major change will be necessary. Most untreated ACOAs prefer the familiarity of a chronic, painful situation. It may be painful, but there is a perceived security since they are used to it. They are terrified of the acute, short term pain of making a healthy change. The reason for this terror is that pain is not the only thing involved. **ACOAs are also being asked to step into the unknown**. This involves self-trust and acting on their own behalf, both of which are often more threatening to them than remaining in a bad situation!

As children in alcoholic families, ACOAs developed a perspective of being trapped. In a very real way, they were. They were powerless to remove themselves or alter the course of the on-going oppression of alcoholism. The best they could do was to defend themselves and await escape to happen to them. **"Happen to them"** is an important phrase. It implies reaction rather than action. They anticipate running away, getting a job at 18, going to college, joining the military, or getting married, instead of initiating and developing their own alternatives. They simply don't have the capacity to engage in an open, honest exploration of their needs, develop alternatives in conjunction with others, and make healthy choices in their own behalf.

ACOA group therapy challenges this framework of waiting for the situation to resolve itself. Acceptance of the unacceptable is no longer an easy or comfortable option. Group members are forced to look at the reality of their situations because the group denies them the luxury of wearing blinders. This challenge to be real usually results in three types of action. Unfortunately, only one of the three is very healthy.

The most common response is to shut down. The ACOA simply retreats. Efforts of fellow group members to engage him are avoided. **The next common response is to terminate therapy.** The issue raised is so threatening that the ACOA leaves instead of facing the need for change. Actually, health can be found in leaving. If the ACOA can be honest and say "I'm leaving because I don't want to look at ..., nor do I want to consider changing it." then at least he leaves with increased self-awareness. If he manufactures an excuse, picks a fight or just disappears not much has been accomplished.

The rarest response is true acceptance of the need for change. Notice I refer to **acceptance** of the need for change. Actual change, when done in a healthy manner, will be a by-product of this acceptance. Change need not happen two seconds after acknowledgment. In fact, instantaneous change can be a kneejerk response which is part of a frantic effort to avoid feelings. In addition to running from the situation, the ACOA is also running from himself when he engages in frantic change. Healthy change results from awareness of self in combination with awareness of the situation. **Healthy change brings the ACOA closer to himself rather than away from a bad situation.** It is a true example of action rather than reaction.

ACOAs resist the need for change in the following areas:

1.   MARRIAGE - A decision for change regarding marriage

does not mean merely staying or leaving. Often the most frightening change is to begin asking for honesty. There is great resistance when ACOAs are asked to identify their needs and communicate them to their spouses, or to determine if their needs are being met and become aware of the emotions involved. **They find it difficult to conceive of actually creating their marriage instead of accepting what's been handed to them.** They also resist healthy fighting, open communication and true interaction. Recovery threatens an ACOA's marriage. ACOAs are being invited to act in their own best interest. The all-or-nothing mentality of ACOAs often makes their marriage a restricted zone. They believe that if they look at it honestly, they will have to leave. There is a tendency toward unilateral and immediate action. The idea of a shared process resulting in slow, steady growth is foreign to them. Often they'll leave group rather than attempt to view their marriage honestly and take appropriate action.

2. FAMILY - The ACOA's desire to protect his family of origin often outweighs his desire to recover. He wants to feel better while not changing the nature of his relationship with his family. It is very difficult for an ACOA to reconstruct this relationship because it requires honesty and vulnerability. He must explicitly make his needs known and set limits and boundaries. This is a step many ACOAs do not want to take. The pain and anger they feel are preferable to not wanting to "hurt" their parents or make them angry. In reality their concern is for their own comfort rather than that of their parents. They do not want to deal with the conflict that a decision to change may cause.

When a member is confronted in this area, his responses are: "I can't. It would crush them." "I'm all they have." "I want to keep the family together." "They need me." This refusal to change is indicative of the fact that the ACOA either doesn't believe his parents are alcoholic or has denied the ramifications of that fact. He views alcoholism not as an illness that robs its victims of the ability to have relationships, but only as a problem the alcoholic has when drinking more than he should.

The ACOA views himself as indispensable to the functioning of a family that is incapable of healthy functioning. To assault this view is to assault a core component of an ACOA's self-concept.

3.   RELATIONSHIPS - ACOAs will be challenged to change many types of relationships. The more "juicy" ones are sexual relationships. We routinely ask ACOAs who are unattached not to date for at least the first six months of treatment. It is common to ask people who have recently broken up with a partner not to date as well. This creates a variety of reactions, ranging from relief to fury. The furious ones are generally those ACOAs who rely on a sexual partner as a means of self-definition. Often when a group member is confronted on continuing an unhealthy sexual relationship, the sequence is rage followed by silence, leading to his either ending the relationship or leaving group.

Other forms of relationships are more subtle, but just as interesting. For example, an ACOA befriends people who are not as smart, socially skilled or gifted as he is. This puts him in the comfortable position of being a big fish in a small pond. He does not have to worry about being challenged by his friends and he can develop a certain sense of superiority. Another type is a person who will not socialize. He is a loner at work who eats by himself and stays alone during his breaks. He won't call group members or partake in group social activities. His actions indicate a lack of commitment to others and a refusal to interact.

Some ACOAs are shaken when pushed to change their behaviors. The thought of reaching out to befriend people who will invite them to grow and become more vulnerable is threatening. Not everyone will accept the challenge to place himself in the fertile ground of interaction rather than the desolate rocks of isolation and encounters.

4.   COMPULSIONS - Eating disorders, compulsive spending, gambling, excessive sleeping, refusal to find a

job and over-working are just some of the areas ACOAs may refuse to confront. To address these areas creates an expectation of change, and often the ACOA does not truly desire change. Change is not easy. A group member may glibly assert he wants to change, but in reality he doesn't. Before change can take place, honesty is necessary. Saying, "I know my eating is a problem, but I don't want to change it" is valuable. Once his fear and defiance are out in the open the ACOA will no longer be able to skate by without taking a stand.

II. PAINFUL AWARENESS - To embrace the truth is all that is required. The word **embrace** is used deliberately. Mere acknowledgment of facts is not enough. More is required than a simple intellectual exercise of identifying and disclosing. An ACOA has generally spent his entire life turning very painful incidents into matter-of-fact occurrences. Embracing reality means not only facing the incidents, but also the emotions they generate. It means the ACOA has to stop and let the impact of his life wash over him. He can no longer repress and homogenize emotions. He must become not just a thinking, but a feeling human being.

This is quite frightening for most ACOAs. It represents a radical departure from the guiding principles of their lives. "Life goes on." "It wasn't that bad." "It's all in the past." "I know it was bad, I'm just happy it's over." "Now that I'm in recovery, what's the use of dredging up all of that?" "They did the best they could." These sentences won't work anymore if the embrace is attempted. The **actual** pain of developing this deep awareness is no where near the **anticipated** pain they have feared. It is this anticipation of pain which causes the "No Trespassing" sign to appear.

In allowing himself to develop an awareness of the pain and shame inside of him, an ACOA must give up control. He must dismantle (or, more accurately, allow to be dismantled) the defenses he has erected to maintain both control of his emotions and the primacy of his intellect. A desperation is born of an unspoken premise that the smallest dent in the dam will result in a deluge. He also must face his fear that if others know these secrets they will come to believe he is essentially unlovable and then leave him. He becomes caught in a bind caused by his misperceptions. If awareness develops, he believes he will lose control and become engulfed by his emotions. Even if his emotions don't get him, he believes his secret will get out and he will be shunned by others. Either way, he perceives he will lose.

The following are some areas that ACOAs will resist looking at in depth.

1. SEXUAL PREFERENCES/FETISHES - Sex in general is often avoided and sexual fetishes (i.e. masochism, exhibitionism, voyeurism, compulsive masturbation) are usually avoided like the plague. When a member is able to take the risk and share deeply regarding a compulsion he has, a cleansing catharsis often follows that not only provides healing for the member but an invitation for the other group members. Sharing on this level is a monumental accomplishment. Refusing to share about sex often results in a major stumbling block to an ACOA's recovery.

2. CHILD ABUSE - There are two levels regarding this issue. ACOAs who were abused as children are becoming more willing to admit that they were. As group progresses, they share more of what happened to them. With some work and encouragement they can generally release the emotions they have repressed for a long time.

We have also found that approximately 50% of ACOAs at our agency have abused or neglected their own children. It is not as easy to address the issue of ACOAs who abuse their own children, but the therapist must be willing to address it when no one else will. Anger and indignation immediately surface when the topic is raised. Members resist sharing the shame of doing to their children what was done to them. They fight admitting the very thing they swore they never would do. They attempt to justify, rationalize and minimize. It is easier for them to admit instances of neglect than to face their feelings regarding that neglect.

Often the ACOA views his own abuse and neglect as **his problem** which he can work on in group, while, at the same time, he completely ignores the needs of his own child. There is a tendency for ACOAs, who so vigorously pursue their own treatment and recovery, not to put the same emphasis on getting help for their children. It is important that the therapist be a knowledgeable guide who can provide resources not only for the ACOA, but for his family as well.

3. PREGNANCIES - Many ACOAs have had or have been involved in pregnancies that resulted in abortion, adoption or desertion. If they decided to raise the child, they might have feelings of anger and hatred toward the child. Often ACOAs have had no outlet for these thoughts and feelings. Frequently they have festered over decades, creating a sense of self-loathing. They view themselves as being failures and horrible people and their response has been to run. If they are able to stop running and embrace reality and do the necessary mourning, then the relief is enormous. However, many are not able to stop running; they often continue running right out of treatment.

4. FAILURE - There are too many possibilities to cite. Instead, I'll give you the principle: **Often ACOAs carry a deep sense of shame for an event or series of events in which they were unable to do the impossible**. ACOAs tend to put impossible burdens on themselves and then feel shame for not living up to these expectations. These failures could be in the area of relationships, ("I should have known my father was going to commit suicide.") employment, ("We lost the contract because I couldn't get my boss to listen to me.") or self-concept, ("That one A- ruined my 4.0 average, I'll never get a job when I graduate."). It takes interaction with others to show ACOAs that these perceptions are unrealistic, otherwise they will remain trapped in a secret world of fear and failure.

Restricted zones are poison. Not addressing them colors an ACOA's entire life. Some improvement in functioning is possible, but recovery is impossible if the "thou shalt nots" remain in place. Ultimately these "no trespassing" signs represent a denial of spirituality. The ACOA says I have decided that I can't bear to address these issues. The I represents an isolation from a Power greater than oneself. It is a repudiation of the second, third and eleventh steps of the AA and Al-Anon programs. The ACOA is saying that he is truly alone and must continue to rely on his own resources. He is unable to take that leap of faith. Once again it is pain that is the ACOA's worst fear and best hope. If he is lucky, the pain of entering these restricted zones will be less than the pain of avoiding them. Unfortunately, pain is a double-edged sword. The pain that leads one ACOA to enter these areas may drive another from treatment. There comes a "now or never" time in ACOA therapy. It varies for each person, but it does come. That is when the therapist, and to a lesser extent the group, must resign the position of accomplice in the maintenance of restricted zones. The issue must be forced. It is important to emphasize that this decision to intervene must be the result of a deliberate, thoughtful process done with much consultation. The decision must be based on the individualized needs of the ACOA and not out of frustration. It is an enormous risk, but to avoid it does a great disservice to the ACOA.

XI. RELAPSE

Relapse is not a popular topic of conversation in the ACOA movement. However, not only does it occur, it occurs quite frequently. This discussion will be limited to how relapse manifests itself in the context of ACOA group therapy. This limitation is helpful because group provides a fairly constant environment, with defined expectations by which we can evaluate an ACOA's behavior. It is valid because an ACOA's participation in group mirrors how he acts outside of group. In general, his behavior during group is more open and honest than it is outside of group.

It is not very useful to discuss relapse without giving it a proper definition. For our purposes, *relapse is defined as a chronic condition which is the result of an ACOA's continued withdrawal from others and increased self-sufficiency. It is characterized by a decrease in self-awareness, honesty and trust. It is also accompanied by a seething anger which is rarely expressed directly and a vaguely defined sense of terror. Relapse is not an isolated incident. It is the culmination of a pattern of behavior.*

It is normal for an ACOA to have periods of decreased participation during the course of his treatment. He may struggle for a couple of weeks before he can address a certain topic. His relationship with group members may be a bit distant for a period of time. These examples do not necessarily indicate relapse. During these "slow" periods it is possible to see a certain **presence** on the part of the ACOA. Even though he is less active, he is present and open to the process. This is in stark contrast to the

64

member who is in relapse. His silence often casts a pall over the room. Other members abide by this silent message of withdrawal and frequently carry on as if he wasn't in the room. (As they get healthy they confront the relapsed member. This causes pressure that often forces the member to make a conscious decision to stay or leave.)

A relapsed member hinders the progress of the ACOA therapy group. Along with his withdrawal, an attitude of defiance is clearly visible. He will not give his peers the satisfaction of interacting with them. Instead he will have encounters based on evasion, feigned ignorance, questioning or hostility. The other members often play into his hands by attempting to help, fix, motivate or encourage the relapsed member. It is not unusual to see most of a session devoted to trying to make the relapsed member see the light. The member twists and dodges, sharing nothing of himself while his peers try harder and harder to reach him.

A member in relapse must be confronted. Even his silence creates disruption. He has refused to accept the gift of themselves that the other group members have presented him; he has rejected their invitation to share himself. It is important to remember that there is a distinction between the new member who is working **towards** interaction, though he has not yet attained it, and the relapsed member who is withdrawing **from** interaction because he does not want to continue to be vulnerable. The key is to address the relapse in a way that does not sacrifice group time in an attempt to change the member's mind. Group members must confront him in order to take care of their own needs. Helping him becomes a secondary consideration. ("You've been pouting for the last six weeks and I'm sick of it. I wish you'd stop screwing around and get honest or else leave." As opposed to "Were you able to get to those extra Al-Anon meetings we talked about last week?")

When a person is in relapse he looks different. He has a physical look of withdrawal. During group he has a far off look in his eyes during his silent periods and a hard look during his encounters. His posture is either rigid or defeated; his tenseness lasts the entire group. He believes an attack is coming and most of his time is spent bracing for it to begin; he is transformed into a controlled, intense, defensive person.

The relapsed member is now isolated and defiant. The battle lines have been drawn. He is mad at the people in group and the people in group are mad at him. It's not a pretty picture. How did it get this far? Where did it all come from? Does it have to be this way? These are crucial questions because they touch the root of the ACOA's dilemma.

Now is the time for another sweeping statement! **Relapse has its foundation in an ACOA's inability to be honest and self-revealing. The inability is based on the mistaken belief that awareness requires instant action, and self-worth is based on performance**. This provides us with the proverbial good news and bad news. The good news is that the simple acts of honesty and self-revelation are the on-going components of recovery. The bad news is that the ACOA has, from a very early age, developed in such a manner as to reduce the opportunities for these acts. The question is whether the ACOA will remain in an environment long enough to have his resistance to honesty and self-revelation dissolved. If he does not, his resistance may become so ingrained that relapse cannot be avoided and once reached will be impossible to overcome.

Relapse often has its beginnings when an ACOA senses that one of his restricted zones is being entered. It doesn't matter which one it is. The point is that he believes something very valuable is being threatened. He believes that he will be **required** to do something he is terrified of doing and something he believes he cannot do. These assumptions make it natural for him to shut down. He has placed himself under impossible pressure, which is internal rather than external. It is the result of those mistaken beliefs regarding self-worth and performance.

The most that ACOA group members can expect from each other is openness, honesty and a willingness to interact. However, individual members put great pressure on themselves. They view their participation in group as an all-or-nothing affair. They believe that they are either doing well, or they are not. If they can't do something perfectly then they won't bother at all! The idea of degrees of progress is foreign to them. This framework of extremes leads to evasiveness, defensiveness and dishonesty because ACOAs can never live up to what they believe is expected of them. It leads to relapse. The best way to examine this further is to look at the two categories of restricted zones in light of the statement regarding the foundation of relapse.

1. AWARENESS - The ACOA's thought process goes like this: "I don't want to look at my relationship with my children. It's too frightening. I wish I could look at it and I also wish I could do it right, but I can't." This attitude results in a personal sense of

failure and a combativeness designed to prevent others from forcing him to face the situation. His mistaken notion is that he has failed in his attempt to embrace the reality of his relationship with his children and that he must defend himself because of that failure.

In fact, just because he is unable to embrace the reality of the relationship totally, does not mean that he has not begun to develop awareness. Nothing could be further from the truth. He has made great strides towards awareness, but he's blind to them! This blindness comes from his inability to accept increments of progress. His all-or-nothing approach traps him in a mistaken sense of failure and forces him to fight with others in an attempt to insulate himself from the anticipated rejection.

Recognizing that he is afraid to look at the relationship with his children is a tremendous step. It means that the ACOA has been able to slow down and experience what is inside of him. It is a sign of progress. It means that he must have some awareness because he realizes he is scared. Actually he may have even more awareness than the ACOA who blabbers on and on about his kids and is totally removed from his emotions. It's great to be really scared and say so. **The trick is to say it as an expression of self rather than an excuse.** It can be a method of sharing himself instead of an expression of defiance. Sadly, the ACOA often passes over or runs from his awareness of fear. It becomes something to hide instead of something to share.

Even more exciting is when the ACOA can say "Because I'm scared, I don't want to talk about it". He discovers that a trap door doesn't open beneath him to dump him out into the street. He is surprised that even though the other members may be disappointed, they appreciate his honesty. It is actually a sign of progress when he can identify what he wants or doesn't want to do and is honest about it. It is so much easier than indirect evasion and resistance. What the ACOA must realize is that by being honest and open about not being able to look at something, he is actually beginning to look at it! **Relapse is caused by secretiveness regarding resistance and an inability to be content with the process of** *developing* **awareness.** All that is required is openness and honesty about what is actually happening inside of him. Problems arise when an ACOA focuses on what **should be** happening and is silent about his resistance. Let's compare this conversation with the thought process previously mentioned.

Member: (looks shaken) "This is tough for me."

Group: "What do you mean?"

Member: "It scares the hell out of me to look at how I am with my kids."

Group: "You really look scared. It's great you know it. Hurray for you!"

Member: "Hurray for me all right, but I don't want to look at it, in fact I don't even want to talk about."

Group: "Even better. Hurray again; we'll move on. However, we want you to do one thing. Next week please let us know how you feel about discussing it. You don't have to discuss it, just let us know if you still don't want to do it."

You mean it's that easy? No, it's that simple. It's far from easy. It involves a life-long pattern of not expressing needs, hiding perceived failures, and repressing all but the most intense emotions. Awareness usually comes in bits and pieces. In group ACOAs spend so much time steeling themselves against being overwhelmed that they overlook the increments of progress. They are often so busy fighting not being knocked off their horses on the way to Damascus (resisting the great flash of awareness) that they ignore the subtle increases in awareness they actually have. In the area of awareness resistance is not the cause of relapse. **Relapse is caused by the denial of resistance and the inability to be open regarding that resistance.**

2. CHANGE - The thought process goes like this: "I know I shouldn't be working 70 hours a week. My spouse and kids are on my back and now Group is going to start in too. If we talk about my working, I know I'll promise to change, but I don't know if I can. I better just lay low." This type of thinking causes problems for the ACOA in two areas. First, it deprives him of an outlet for sharing his family problems, his internal emptiness and the emotions generated by compulsive working. Second, it puts him in a battle with his fellow group members whom he perceives as attempting to force him to do what he is incapable of doing. The primary root of both problems is his belief that his self-worth and intrinsic value are based on his ability to change certain behaviors and perform in a certain way.

There is an assumption that a problem can't be discussed unless it is resolved in advance. This ACOA's perspective is that a problem is discussed to inform group about something that **has** happened instead of seeking their help for something that **is** happening. He asks for help only when help is not actually needed. Help can be sought only when it is **not** a fundamental necessity. ("I only have 10 people to help me clean up after the party and I want to ask if you'll also stay and help clean up." as opposed to "This separation hurts so much I'm afraid to be myself. Can I please come over on Saturday?")

Believing that group members will judge him as harshly as he judges himself, he withdraws. Work becomes a problem that he has to carry by himself. Remember that the ACOA generally operates to minimize losses and prevent rejection. It is foreign for him to operate by moving toward others. As a result, the pressure builds. He becomes angry with his spouse, distant from his kids, resentful at work. Each time he is in group he becomes briefly aware of how terrible his life is and how much he has to hide. He must put a wall around his true self and put on a pleasant face to the group. He begins to live a lie.

He believes that sharing will result in pressure rather than relief. He expects to be bludgeoned into action that he is incapable of undertaking. **He thinks he can't reveal what is happening to him unless he is already capable of changing**. This concept of change is reflective of isolation and self-sufficiency. This ACOA is unaware that he can be helped. He is unable to see that honesty and self-revelation increase his ability to change, that it is not necessary for him to rely solely on his own means. Implicit in all of this is the erroneous assumption that people are attracted to the ACOA because of his strengths and achievements. In fact, deep attraction is usually based on transparency and vulnerability. "This is who I am, warts and weaknesses included."

Another mistaken notion is that change must be instantaneous. In most cases change is a by-product of true awareness, openness and honesty. It is a result of continued efforts to share with, and enlist the aid of, others. As awareness grows, the ability to harm oneself, or others, decreases. Change is the result of a process; it cannot be done on demand. (There are, however, some areas where external change must be demanded regardless of internal process. This is true primarily in critical areas such as incest and violence.)

This is not to say that the group won't push the ACOA to act, or that they won't be angry regarding a lack of progress. This anger, however, has nothing to do with personal rejection. It does not mean the ACOA is worthless. Mistakes and lack of progress have nothing to do with self-worth. **Honesty and interaction are the primary factors the ACOA must seek.** Members will experience a full range of emotions and will have a lot of things to resolve as the process of change continues. The important thing is that there will be no secrets. Everyone will know where everyone else stands. In this case, the ACOA's compulsive working will become an on-going legitimate area of discussion. His progress or lack of progress will be discussed on a continuing basis. **This guarantees change.**

Relapse does not result from fear of awareness or an inability to change. Relapse is the result of the on-going denial of that fear and inability, coupled with withdrawal and a retreat into self-sufficiency. Mistakes and failures are essential to an ACOA's recovery. It is the fear of mistakes and failures which is responsible for most of an ACOA's difficulty in group! **Similarly, relapse is not caused by resistance.** It is caused by an inability to be honest regarding that resistance. Resistance is natural and necessary. The variables emerge from what is done with resistance. Will they lead to relapse or surrender?

Relapse is more serious than resistance. Once an ACOA is in relapse he usually leaves treatment. It's as if a private battle has been silently fought and a decision is made to retreat. Intellectual arguments or browbeating will not keep the person in group. Ironically, the very thing that scares the ACOA away may be the one thing that will entice him to stay, or eventually return. **It is the joyful and terrifying experience of being touched deeply by other caring ACOAs.** The member's time in group has been characterized by confrontation and invitation. He was invited to be real and was confronted on his rejection of the invitation. This is the combination which makes him want to run, but also plants the subtle seeds of hope and change.

The only chance a relapsed ACOA has to continue growing is to talk with others. If he can talk honestly about the fear and seething anger he is experiencing, then he may be able to stay and continue his journey of recovery. Even if he does not stay, his decision to leave becomes an open one that will have some benefit for him and not cause him much damage. Leaving in silence is a mere reaction; a sign of the ACOA's lack of health. It is self-defeating, having no other result than to perpetuate his isolation. As with most other things in ACOA group therapy, the decision to leave is secondary to how it is made. **The act of leaving is not as**

important as how that act is shared!

What are the consequences of relapse? Are those who terminate better or worse off than when they started? When an ACOA who is also a recovering alcoholic relapses, does it also jeopardize his sobriety? Is relapse inevitable and in some cases necessary? Why do some ACOAs recover while others do not? I'm not going to attempt to answer these questions now (partly because I don't have answers to most of them); it is more important that they be raised. In discussing relapse and raising such questions, we are moving forward. We are leaving the honeymoon stage of the ACOA movement and focusing on the tough issues of treatment and relapse. Asking such questions acknowledges the seriousness of the ACOA syndrome and emphasizes that there are no easy answers or cures.

XII. AWARENESS

Awareness is different from factual knowledge. This concept must be understood because it is the foundation of this chapter. Awareness is a spiritual rather than a mental process. While factual knowledge deals with information and events in a physical or mental realm, awareness provides a true vision in which a person experiences something as it actually is. Knowledge is incomplete and often illusory. Awareness is whole and essentially revealing. A person can have knowledge, yet be completely unaware. **It seems as if all resistance in ACOAs is aimed at evading awareness**. The example of a man blind from birth can help illuminate this distinction: a blind person can know the facts about the color blue. He may know the fact that blue is darker than white and lighter than black. He may know that the sky is blue and that blue is often the preferred color of Catholic School uniforms. At the same time we can truthfully say that this blind person has no awareness of the color blue. He can speak about it, but he has no experience of it. He is essentially removed from it. He knows facts about the color blue, but he does not "know" the color blue. **He has no awareness**.

What does this have to do with ACOAs? The reason for this brief foray into epistemology is that the awareness/knowledge distinction is crucial to an ACOA's therapeutic and recovery process. As long as ACOAs stay in the realm of knowledge the realities of their lives will be blunted and there will be no imperative for them to begin the painful process of fundamental change. Knowledge (information) provides ACOAs with the language of recovery but does not provide its substance. Knowledge is seductive for ACOAs. It holds forth the false promise of self-adjustment based on intellectual information. It disguises the fact that recovery requires a transformation as opposed to a mere rearranging of thoughts and perceptions.

It is not unusual to see ACOAs expounding upon their character defects, childhood traumas and lack of intimacy to whomever will listen. The reason for this enthusiastic, though indiscriminating, disclosure is the excitement of developing a new data base of information regarding themselves. Most ACOAs have fragmented and incomplete memories of their early years. When ACOAs get together, they discover that not only do they have a "history" or "story" of their own, but they also share a commonality of experience with millions of others. This sharing of stories, besides enabling them to bond with others, enables them to fill in the blanks and join together the pieces of their own individual stories.

Unfortunately, ACOAs in treatment often become stuck in the "information phase". They continue to **think** about their histories and in turn they share these thoughts with other group members. Their newly discovered knowledge provides a comfortable arena from which they can operate. They can safely interact on an intellectual level, sharing their thoughts instead of their true selves.

ACOAs use knowledge in order to avoid awareness. Knowledge fosters an ACOA's sense of control. It provides him with the opportunity to gather data and then analyze, debate, structure, rearrange, add or subtract, filter and correlate it in a manner of his own choosing. He is removed from what he knows and where he has been. His true self is hidden behind a wall of information. Staying behind this wall, he can have encounters that preclude vulnerability and allow him to maintain control.

Knowledge requires active effort. Often, in ACOA therapy groups, one can envision a Wizard of Oz type of experience. Members hide behind their curtains frantically pulling levers, throwing switches and turning cranks, in order to create a public image which they believe is more acceptable than who they truly are. **ACOAs strive to be correct, act appropriately and find the right answer.** They work hard to restructure what they know in order to present an image which they believe fulfills the dictates of a particular situation.

Two examples of ACOAs attempting to avoid awareness in

73

group therapy are **"Helping"** and **"Sharing data"**. These defenses can best be viewed by using the following example:

An ACOA is talking about remembering that he was sexually abused by his mother. He is tapping into a great deal of intense emotion. It is a very moving and powerful scene.

1. "The helper", being other-focused, immediately starts talking. He lets the member know that the incest wasn't his fault. He begins to explain the dynamics of incest. He asks the member what his relationship with his mother is like today and what he plans to do to resolve it. At the end he thanks the member for sharing the incest and tells him how well he did.

The helper's response is designed to place himself in a position of safety and superiority. He is happy to focus on and help the incest victim, because it means that he does not have to become aware of himself. He automatically slips into a well practiced method of keeping emotion and vulnerability at bay. He approaches this person as if they were both participants in an exercise designed to develop the proper response to a particular problem. The only risk he takes is that the incest victim may get mad at one of his questions, comments or suggestions. This is preferable to looking at the anger he may be carrying around regarding his own mother. He can give the appearance of participation and involvement with no risk of his true self being broached.

2. "The sharer" says "Me too," and then becomes quiet. He states in a matter-of-fact fashion that his mother abused him 3 times. Although he shares this information so that the other victim will know that he is not alone, he has no desire to do any processing of the incest. He knows that it's important that he let the group know this information about his background, but that's as far as he's willing to go.

This ACOA shares data rather than himself. He is willing to acknowledge the fact of the incest, but he is unwilling to become aware of the reality behind that fact. Disclosing the fact at this particular time actually results in shutting the door on awareness! His bland disclosure almost certainly will be passed over as group members are more focused on, and attracted to, the spontaneous, emotionally honest sharing of the original incest victim. The sharer has provided information about a painful event in a manner that precludes addressing the pain. He believes he has fulfilled his responsibility to himself and the group and has no more work to do in this area.

74

Resistance to awareness results in ACOAs discovering more facts or knowledge about themselves while still remaining in blindness. It is important to note that often ACOAs have no idea that they are blind. They operate under the assumption that facts and knowledge are the sum of their universe. They cannot conceive that knowledge is only 25% of the whole picture and that they are missing the other three quarters. They are blind to their own blindness!

An ACOA cannot be **made** to become aware. However, he can benefit by being shown the limitations of facts and knowledge! This is why an active, knowledgeable therapist and concerned, committed fellow group members are so important. By interacting with and watching others, the ACOA begins to realize that there is more to him than his knowledge. The example of others, along with their confrontation, will provide an invitation to the ACOA to venture out from his protected fiefdom of facts to discover the world of awareness.

This is not an easy process, nor is it guaranteed to be successful. An ACOA's original retreat from awareness and into knowledge was the result of the pain and trauma of being raised by active alcoholics. **This retreat was a reasonable response to an absolutely unreasonable situation**. This trauma and turmoil covered most, if not all, of his developmental stages and became his main point of reference. Giving up these defenses will mean an ACOA must become aware of the very things he has been running from his entire life. This is not easily done. It entails a long painful process which requires not only great courage and stamina on the part of the ACOA, but faith as well.

What is this "awareness" that ACOAs resist so tenaciously? It is easier to say what awareness is not, rather than what it actually is. It is not facts, knowledge, information, descriptions, understanding or identification. **Awareness has been described as a true vision**. It is when a person experiences a thing, another person or himself as they actually are. This description implies depth, richness and thoroughness of vision. **Awareness is complete**. When an ACOA becomes aware he is touched at depth. Awareness creates a unity where a person experiences a connection with both himself and the world. **Awareness removes the walls of knowledge**.

Most ACOAs view recovery as a process they must undertake that involves knowledge, hard work and discipline. As a result of their work in group, they expect to develop enough insight and skill to change themselves in a desired manner. Recovery is considered a product resulting from their efforts. It is something they reach, capture, or create. (Please notice that these are all active words. Their assumption is that recovery is essentially a self-directed process under their control.) Others may help by being supportive, confrontative, or informative, but the individual is essentially alone as he weighs all the options and makes the decisions. His task is to find out what is wrong with himself and then correct it. This process requires very little fundamental change on the part of the ACOA. In reality, it is a formula for improvement rather than recovery. The ACOA's guiding principle "I must maintain control" is left intact while he rearranges his knowledge and method of operating. This can result in significant improvement regarding his encounters with other people. He may come to realize that he need not work seventy hours a week, he doesn't have to visit his parents when he doesn't want to, he can set limits for himself and there is nothing wrong with having fun. These improvements are not to be taken lightly. They represent significant relief for the ACOA and enhance his life. **Settling for improvement is not failure, but we must remember improvement is not recovery!**

ACOAs who view therapy as an information gathering and self-adjustment process are said to be improving instead of recovering because they have no awareness. They are focused on what they **do** instead of **who they are**. They want to **make** something happen instead of **letting** something occur. They are willing to **change things** instead of **being open to who they are**. They are still searching for the "right" answer. The focus is still external. Their goal is to figure something out as opposed to truly experiencing it.

Awareness is not active. It cannot be forced or made to happen. It is a by-product of an ACOA's surrender. As long as he is still fighting to change, improve, fix, understand, forgive, etc., awareness is impossible. The ACOA who is pursuing these things is actually running from himself. He is blind to the **I** "behind the curtain" who is still struggling in the Land of Oz to keep control and pull the right lever. An ACOA must stop and do nothing (no thing). It is very difficult to hit a moving target and the ACOA has had a good deal of practice in constantly moving. He must stop fighting and become aware of what he is fighting and running from.

ACOAs cannot grab awareness. The best they can do is desire it. This concept is alien to most ACOAs who enter group. They are eager to work and learn. They are ready to **do** something or have something **done** to them. This attitude is not surprising in a population that by necessity has become self-sufficient and task oriented on the one hand, or sickly dependent and passive on the other. Conflict arises when they discover that recovery is not something they can do or something that will be given to them from the outside.

ACOAs must stop **trying** to develop awareness. **Attempting to develop awareness is another method of camouflaging control.** Control is manifested in the attempt to determine in what areas the awareness should be focused. Even though the ACOA claims he is actively seeking awareness, he is doing it on his own terms with his illness as his main source of reference. He still believes that he can shape and direct the process. It becomes a self-propelled journey through a limited area. He instinctively avoids the many restricted zones to which he is blind. The result is that he has merely rearranged his perceptions and actions while avoiding basic transformation.

Our friend the blind man again illustrates our point:

He is very excited because an operation has given him his sight. Even though the operation was a success, he still keeps his eyes closed because he's used to his world of darkness. However, he is becoming dissatisfied with his life because he has a vague sense that he is missing out on a lot of things and he also feels isolated and lonely. One day he finally gets enough courage to see his doctor. The doctor tells him that the answer to all his problems is the color blue; if he can become aware of this color, he will be in great shape. So the ex-blind man does what he was progammed to do his entire life. He interviews dye makers, listens to songs, attends lectures, reads about it in braille, and even goes to Memphis to learn to sing the blues. In fact, he learns so much that, he becomes a noted scholar and teaches others about the color blue as well.

All the while he is doing pretty well, making good money, travelling, and meeting nice people. His life has really improved but when he is alone and able to be quiet he becomes afraid, because he knows something is missing. To fill that void, he studies even more and spends his free time helping others and passing on his knowledge. Still, his unhappiness increases and he becomes desperate.

In his despair he returns to his doctor and tells him how hard he has tried to know the color blue. Having used every ounce of willpower and determination, his anquish is deep because he knows every fact about the color blue and is still lost, lonely and afraid. Worse yet, he cannot work anymore. He has given up and doesn't know what else to do.

The doctor takes him by the arm and gently leads him outside.

"Open your eyes."
The man is stunned.
"Just open your eyes."
The man slowly opens his eyes and looks up at the sky.
"This is the color blue."
The man is amazed. "I worked so hard to learn about blue, yet I never knew it at all. All I had to do was open my eyes! It just never occurred to me."
Now that he has become aware of the color blue his whole life is put into a different perspective. All his theories are now meaningless. What he had valued so much is actually worthless. All he had to do was open his eyes; nothing more and nothing less.

When ACOAs try to "get" awareness, they rely on their unhealthy perceptions and methods of operating. Their active search is biased and colored. It becomes yet another variation on a familiar theme. There is no real openness in this process. **The primary task of ACOAs is to want or desire awareness**. They often prefer to scurry around trying to develop awareness rather than truly desiring it. To desire awareness there must be a commitment to be open, and a willingness to follow that vision wherever it goes. ACOAs often answer rationally when asked if they want awareness. They are quick to say "Yes, of course we do." Once in treatment they discover that they had answered much too quickly!

Awareness is profoundly beautiful and liberating, but it involves great pain and an imperative for healthy behavior. Do ACOAs want to be aware of the reality of their childhoods, their relationships, their emotions and their defenses? Resistance comes into play because at first awareness can only be handled in small increments. The biggest resistance to awareness is ACOAs' belief that they are fundamentally unlovable. The driving force behind most of the defenses and pathologies of ACOAs is lack of self-worth and self-acceptance. "If you knew who I really was, you'd leave me." "If I make a mistake, I'll die." "I have to stay with her because I'm terrified to leave." "If I don't work hard, no one will want me." "I can't go because they need me." The list goes on and on because ACOAs lead lives of reaction rather than action. They operate to prevent people from leaving instead of moving closer to others. ACOAs define themselves by externals and are removed from their sense of self. At their core is an unfulfilled yearning for love, coupled with a sense of unworthiness.

ACOAs run from this sense of unworthiness. Their over-achievements and hyper-vigilance are designed to compensate for this radical lack of self-worth. They hide from themselves and others their fundamental belief that they are failures. **ACOAs do not see awareness as liberating**. Instead they view it as a painful confirmation of a dark truth they are trying to avoid. They are afraid to feel all that is inside of them. ACOAs' fear of awareness is based upon the unspoken assumption that it will cause their tightly wound balance of denial, performance, achievement, unexpressed needs, repressed emotion and external focus to collapse. Slowing down and becoming aware is threatening because it calls an ACOA to experience his life of emptiness instead of continually reacting to it.

   "Unconditional self-worth" is often only a concept to ACOAs. Nothing in the usual alcoholic family can give children this gift. As a result they develop a structure of skills, talents and assets around a hollow core of emptiness and devaluation. This structure is designed to substitute external focus, performance, and striving for internal awareness and self-love. They can talk about it, discuss techniques for getting it or even claim to have it. Unless they receive help, the best they can do is act as if they have it.

   What can lead an ACOA to awareness? My own thought is that **awareness is actually spirituality**. It results from saying "yes" to the gift of a Higher Power, which allows us to experience our innate connection with others. This gift is a realization that an ACOA is good, valuable and lovable in and of himself. He becomes able to see that there is nothing he can do to make himself more worthy of love. This gift of awareness (spirituality) erases the need to create a mask of performance and accomplishment. The ACOA no longer needs to perform in order to be connected with others. He only needs to open his eyes and say "yes" to the connection that is already there.

   How can an ACOA say "yes" to this gift? ACOA group therapy in conjunction with self-help group participation provides a fertile ground for awareness to develop. They provide the twin seeds of pain and nurturance that the ACOA needs. Pain (hitting bottom) is necessary because without it there would be no reason for an ACOA to change or even to realize that he is more numb than alive. It is necessary to experience and be aware of emotional pain before it can be resolved. When an ACOA runs from or represses emotional pain he actually feeds it and fosters isolation from his true self. His defenses are so fortified and entrenched that it takes a great deal of pain before he will consider raising the white flag of surrender.

ACOAs dread surrender. (Deep down, often hidden, they have a quiet yearning for it as well.) When the moment of surrender takes place, it is usually accompanied by terror. At this instant the seed of nurturance takes hold. Other ACOAs invite the ACOA, tottering on the brink of surrender, to let go. They have accepted him over a period of months and years despite his resistance, affirming him time and time again when he was unable to affirm himself. Their care, shown by their willingness to confront him, express their emotion to him and share themselves with him, has given him hope. This slow infusion of affirmation has created a safety net as he leaps into the dark surrender.

As we discussed in the relapse chapter, these seeds do not always take root. Often ACOAs are simply unable to accept the gift of awareness. They sense the terror as their barriers begin to erode, and flee before they experience liberation. Resistance to awareness is to be expected; it is not something an ACOA can overcome. Rather **it is something that falls away when an ACOA stops running and lets go of his fear**. Well, this sounds pretty nice, but I still haven't shown exactly how an ACOA lets go. Perhaps the last chapter will point us in the right direction, even if it cannot give us the definitive answer.

XIII. RECOVERY

In the beginning of this tome, recovery was defined as true awareness coupled with the ability to have healthy intimate relationships. It's time to give the definition substance by becoming more specific. It is important that the reader be aware of the limitations (some would say folly) of this attempt. It is very easy to say what recovery is not. (i.e. It is not mere improvement, increased knowledge, idealizing the past, or developing a language of psycho-babble.) To describe recovery we are shackled because we must use **words** (realm of knowledge) to describe **awareness** (not of the realm of knowledge). Words are not the complete truth. I'm merely using them to point to the truth. Recovery can only be recognized by seeing it in others or experiencing it in yourself. **You will know it when you see it**. With that caveat in place I will now proceed to ignore it and give you the "definitive chapter" on recovery!

Recovery has at least five essential aspects. They cannot be viewed as goals or destinations. They are all process-oriented and constantly evolving. They are the antithesis of the all-or-nothing, win-or-lose, succeed-or-fail mentality expressed by ACOAs in the chapter on relapse. **These aspects have as their premise the belief that ACOAs are intrinsically good and lovable but they are blind to their self-worth.**

1. ACOAS MUST WANT TO RECOVER. This is not as self-

evident as it appears. Most ACOAs enter treatment wanting to feel better. Instead of viewing the pain and discomfort of a particular situation as symptomatic of a larger problem in general, they focus their efforts on alleviating the pain. They develop a short term strategy which ignores the long-term problem. Their desire is to change a situation or their reaction to it. (i.e. "I want to learn how to feel good about my job even though my employer doesn't appreciate me.") They do not want to call into question their entire method of operating.

An ACOA will recover when he truly wants to. "When the student is ready, the master will appear" applies to ACOAs very well. What makes them ready to recover and **want** to become aware? It is impossible to say. Recovery can be described as **seeing yourself and the world with different eyes**. There are no changes other than that the blind man can now see. To be **tired of** your present situation and reactions is simply exchanging one stale method of control for another; to **want to** recover (true desire) requires a spiritual transformation.

2. ACOAS MUST EXPERIENCE THEIR EMOTIONS. ACOAs must experience and become aware of their emotions; past and present. This is different from understanding. analyzing, dismissing or wallowing in them. **They must face the repressed emotions they have avoided facing since childhood.**

They cannot be content with knowledge of their childhood. They must become aware of their childhood so they can experience it and let it go. ACOAs are afraid to enter this warehouse of repressed emotions because they are afraid of being overwhelmed and ruled by them. **They are unaware that they are being ruled by these emotions at this very moment!** In fact, awareness can only result in freedom and the possibility of a life of action as opposed to reaction.

At the same time, awareness of present day emotions adds a richness to the lives of ACOAs. People cannot selectively numb emotions. If anger and sorrow are repressed, so are happiness and joy. Awareness allows ACOAs to experience each emotion and then move on. Awareness of emotions leads both to self-honesty and honesty with others. ACOAs are no longer forced to use a variety of ploys and manipulations to conceal their emotions from themselves and others. Emotions are simply emotions instead of harbingers of a deluge!

3. ACOAS MUST TAKE RISKS AND BE OPEN WITH OTHERS. Recovery is achieved in community with others. Awareness allows ACOAs to experience the fact that they do not have to distort themselves by providing "the correct response", not making waves, and not expressing needs to others. They will discover that they are not dependent on others for their self-worth; they become free to be honest. Self-acceptance enables them to accept others as they are, without having to recreate them to suit a fantasy image.

Awareness allows ACOAs to act honestly and openly with others. They become free from blind, automatic reactions resulting from repressed emotions, unexpressed needs and an inability to set limits. They give up their quest for a perfect relationship that will make them whole. Awareness enables ACOAs to experience their own worth and lovableness; they need not place the burden on others to make them whole. As an ACOA recovers he becomes free to take more risks in relationships. He realizes he does not have to cling to them. Making a mistake is not the end of the world. He understands that if a relationship cannot tolerate honesty, then it is not worth having. As a result, his relationships lose predictability and develop a new richness. They become living organisms that are constantly changing and growing while the underlying principles of acceptance and honesty remain.

4. RECOVERY REQUIRES ACCEPTANCE OF SELF. **Awareness spawns self-acceptance; it brings spiritual peace**. Awareness results in a person making friends with both his assets and his liabilities. Change begins to happen automatically as a by-product of awareness with no effort on his part. This concept is foreign to most ACOAs. They are devoted to two tasks: **working** extremely hard to improve themselves and control events, while **running** from those parts of themselves too painful to explore. These tasks require planning and action directed by the ACOA.

Awareness is radically different from these tasks. **It does**

not require ACOAs to change. Change begins automatically once awareness is developed. It is outside of their control. In other words, recovery is not something ACOAs do. **It is something that happens to them**. Recovery comes from their awareness, not from their efforts. They are being asked to not only let go of various defects, but to let go of a lifetime of self-sufficiency. They must place themselves in the hands of others and a Higher Power. **The task of ACOAs is not to recover. Instead, their task is not to stop recovery from happening!**

Awareness decreases the pressure to change. Once the pressure is gone, transformation can occur. Once the ACOA resigns as Chairman of the Universe and Captain of his Recovery, recovery can truly happen. There is no longer a need for the success or failure mentality and the causes of shame are removed. The focus is no longer on changing behavior, because, at root, this is an egocentric activity. The focus instead is on awareness and its natural consequence, transformation.

5. RECOVERY REQUIRES THE TOTAL COMMITMENT OF AN ACOA'S ENTIRE BEING. Alcoholics Anonymous has a number of powerful phrases and sayings that can be applied to ACOAs. "We stood at the turning point." "We beg of you to be fearless and thorough from the very start." "Half measures availed us nothing." "The results were nil until we let go absolutely." "Deflation of ego in depth." They all call for a total commitment to recovery. It is somewhat easier for alcoholics than ACOAs to develop that commitment because the spectre of a return to drinking looms over them. ACOAs are not so fortunate since they do not have that tangible, physical presence. (An exception is ACOAs who are also recovering alcoholics; if they do not take care of their ACOA illness, their alcoholism may flare up and take care of it for them!)

ACOAs cannot afford to view treatment as a luxury. If they do, they will not stay around long enough for recovery to have a chance to happen. **A treatment plan consisting of ACOA group therapy once a week will not work**. It will increase their level of discomfort, but not enough to provide any healthy resolution. They will have no resources to deal with the pain that inevitably occurs upon hitting bottom. A minimal commitment will cause them to work hard to avoid hitting bottom and as a result their pain will actually be prolonged.

There is no way an ACOA can truly benefit from treatment at this level of investment. He will deal with the pain by either leaving or shutting down emotionally. An ACOA can do two things to enhance his chances of recovery. The first is to pray for willingness. This is different from **trying** to be willing; it is asking a Higher Power (God or other people) for help. It is the beginning of openness when an ACOA asks for help in this area.

The second is to show up at a lot of places. Weekly therapy, daily meetings, daily phone calls and socializing with other members all provide nurturance for the ACOA and an environment for the seeds of recovery to grow. This intense time commitment allows him to create a lifestyle conducive to recovery. It is a physical sign of his commitment to recovery.

This is not to say that an ACOA is obligated to be totally willing to address every issue and change every thing. **Resistance is natural and even healthy because it shows that the recovery process is being taken seriously and hitting close to home.** An ACOA is obligated to place himself in an atmosphere where willingness can develop. He must do the leg work. Relapse cannot resist total commitment and honesty. However, if an ACOA only has minimal attendance and will not look at, or even discuss, his level of willingness, then recovery cannot resist relapse.

Recovery is internal rather than external. It is composed of surrender and transformation, as opposed to working hard and changing. It results in making friends with one's character defects instead of making great efforts to get rid of them. (Again we see the wisdom of AA. The sixth and seventh steps call on God to remove character defects instead of having the individual direct that process.) It can best be done in an environment where recovery is primary and there is a kernel of willingness to be open. Recovery cannot be charted by a score card or check list. When it does occur, it is readily visible to the ACOA and others. The person becomes transparent. The struggle is over and what remains is awareness, unity with others, and most of all, self-love.

XIV. CONCLUSION

This book attempted to deal with such problems as resistance, the threat of recovery, relapse and the fear of self-discovery. Though these topics are disturbing and do not lend themselves to easy answers, they also provide a good deal of excitement. Recovery is not a result of an individual's working very hard to change himself! The problems discussed in this book are merely obstacles to awareness. The task is not to change the obstacles or character defects, but to become truly aware of them. The ACOA is being asked to accept himself as he is. In fact, once he becomes friends with his defects, they will automatically fall away!

These problems can be seen as layers of cataracts. All that is necessary is to let each layer drop off and accept the corresponding increase in awareness. **The ACOA just has to show up, and want to be willing and open to awareness**. This sounds quick and easy, but in reality it is enormously difficult and there will be many opportunities for an individual to close himself to the process. Awareness is liberating, but the **thought** of it is terrifying. That is why "thinking" is so often counter-productive for ACOAs. Thinking about awareness causes fear. **This is because the thoughts of untreated ACOAs regarding self-worth, self-acceptance and the reality of their relationships are, as a result of the nature of their illness, superficial and/or distorted**. They need to see, not understand, things differently. They need to accept the "new eyes" offered to them by their fellow ACOAs. Awareness and recovery are to be experienced, not analyzed.

They are gifts that ACOAs need only accept. Nothing more is required.

This book is based on the ideas of many people who have influenced and formed the foundation of my thoughts. In all likelihood 25% of my thinking will change by the time this book is in print. Even so, these books are both worthwhile and provocative.

1. deMello, A., **The Song of the Bird**, Gujarat Sahitya Prakash, Anand, Gujarat, India, 1982.
2. Krishnamurti, J., **Think on These Things**. Harper and Row, New York, N.Y., 1964
3. Neil, A.S., **Summerhill**. Hart Publishing Co., New York, N.Y. 1960.
4. **Alcoholics Anonymous,** Alcoholics Anonymous World Services, New York, N.Y., 3rd edition, 1976.
5. Brown, S., Presentation, NYS Coalition for Children of Alcoholic Families Conference, October, 1984.
6. Cermak, T., and Brown, S. "International Group Therapy with the Adult Children of Alcoholics", **International Journal of Group Psychotherapy,** 1982, 32C37.

Finally, I'd like to close with a story told by Tony deMello, SJ. In a couple of paragraphs it says what has taken me several chapters to say:

One ocean fish stopped another and said "Excuse me but you are wiser and more experienced than I, and I hope you'll be able to help me. Could you tell me where I might find this thing they call the Ocean? I've been searching for a long time but I haven't been able to find it."

The wiser fish said "You are swimming in it now. This is the Ocean."

"This can't be it. This is only water. I'm searching for **the Ocean**" said the young fish as he swam away, disappointed but intent on continuing his search.